Just Seeing

Insight Meditation and Sense-Perception

by

Cynthia Thatcher

Buddhist Publication Society
P.O. Box 61
54 Sangharaja Mawatha
Kandy
Sri Lanka
http://www.bps.lk

Published in 2008
Revised Edition: 2011

National Library of Sri Lanka - Cataloguing in Publication data

Thatcher, Cynthia
Just Seeing: Insight Meditation & Sense - Perception / Cynthia Thatcher.-ed. by Bhikkhu Nyanatusita.- Kandy: Buddhist Publication Society Inc., 2008.- p.146; 21cm
ISBN 978-955-24-0320-0   Price: Rs.

i. 294.34435 DDC 21   ii. Title
  iii. Bhikkhu Nyanatusita-ed.
  1. Meditation   2. Buddhism

Typeset at the BPS in URW Palladio Pali

Printed by
Ajith Printers (Pvt) Ltd.
342, Old Kesbewa Road, Rattanapitiya,
Boralesgamuwa, Sri Lanka.
Tel: +94 (0) 112517269

Namo tassa bhagavato arahato samma sambuddhassa
Namo tassa bhagavato arahato samma sambuddhassa
Namo tassa bhagavato arahato samma sambuddhassa

When you see, just see. When you hear, just hear. When you think, just think; and when you know, just know.

—Saṃyutta Nikāya 35:95

CONTENTS

Author's Preface

The following terms are used interchangeably: *paramattha dhamma*, *nāma-rūpa*, and ultimate reality. Also used synonymously are the expressions: *sammuti-sacca*, conventional reality, and conventional truth.

The painting mentioned in this book is *A Sunday Afternoon on the Island of La Grande Jatte* (1884-1886), by the nineteenth-century Neo-impressionist French master Georges-Pierre Seurat. "Pointillism," for readers unfamiliar with the term, is a painting technique in which pigment is applied in dots. When seen from a distance they merge into recognizable shapes and secondary colors.

This book was inspired by Mahāsi Sayādaw's work, *A Discourse on Mālukyaputta Sutta*. For the extraordinary wisdom of my vipassanā and Abhidhamma teacher, Achan Sobin Namto (Ven. Sopako Bodhi Bhikkhu), I am deeply grateful. Without his knowledge this book would not have been possible. My sincere gratitude and thanks go to Bhikkhu Nyanatusita of the BPS, Ven. Bhikkhu Bodhi, Ashin Otama, Sister Dharmapālī, Dr. Carola Andujo, Morley Chalmers, Nina van Gorkom, Jim Mooney, and Margarita Thatcher for their valuable criticism, comments and suggestions. I would also like to thank John Bullitt for kindly explaining different systems of sutta enumeration. Any mistakes are due to my own ignorance.

—C.T.

Preface by Achan Sobin Namto

I was very pleased to learn that my long-time student, Cynthia Thatcher, had written a superb book about seeing things as they really are. In these pages she demonstrates a keen intellect and penetrative understanding of the Dhamma. At the same time, the Buddha's deeper teachings are brought to life through the skillful use of description and metaphor. I am very proud of her achievement.

Part of this book's appeal is the writing style. Ven. Bhikkhu Bodhi, after reading an early version of the manuscript, remarked, "*Just Seeing* is beautifully written. This woman really knows how to write." Cynthia has a B.A. in philosophy from Reed College and an M.A. in English from the University of Colorado. These two aspects of her background come together in this book, as she is often able to render subtle philosophic concepts in lyrical prose that will be easily understood by most readers.

I first met Cynthia in 1993, when she practiced intensive vipassana for over three months at my meditation center in Colorado. During that time she acquired a good experience of insight meditation. Since then she has attended retreats in the U.S., Thailand, and India. She also studied Abhidhamma under my guidance.

Cynthia has been my assistant since 1994. I always found her to be extremely intelligent in her understanding of the Dhamma. In 1998 I chose her to be co-presenter, and co-author, of a keynote speech I was invited to give to the International Association of Lions Clubs. Recently she has written for the award-winning periodical, *Tricycle: The Buddhist Review*. With my blessing, she now teaches meditation online in the Dhamma Friend Program.

Because of my confidence in her knowledge, I appointed her Director of the Vipassana Dhura Meditation Society (www.vipassanadhura.com), a nonprofit corporation I established in 1986. Cynthia is truly a great asset to Buddhism, not only in the U.S., her birthplace, but in the world. I believe that her tireless contributions to the Dhamma will help authentic Theravada Buddhism develop in the West.

I highly recommend *Just Seeing* because it explains the essence of vipassana, which is to see things as they are. May the merit gained from her book, and the merit I have performed throughout my entire life, contribute to Cynthia's good health and future progress in the Dhamma.

Achan Sobin Namto (Sopako Bodhi Bhikkhu)
19 September, 2008
Bangkok, Thailand

INTRODUCTION

The way in which we experience sights, sounds and other sense-impressions is directly relevant to the goal of liberation from suffering. Perceiving a sight or sound with mindfulness can move us toward happiness, whereas the same image or sound, viewed with delusion, can entangle the mind in distress. This book looks at the role of sense-perception in insight meditation, explaining how sense-data can be known so as to eliminate pain and lead to awakening.

Insight meditation (*vipassanā*) aims at seeing reality as it actually is. "When you see," the Buddha said, "just see. When you hear, just hear. When you think, just think; and when you know, just know." ("Knowing" includes smelling, tasting and touching.) The eminent Burmese teacher Mahāsi Sayādaw called this passage, "insight meditation in a nutshell." This concentrated teaching appears in several places in the Pali Canon of Theravada Buddhism, most notably the Bāhiya and Mālukyaputta suttas.

Bāhiya and Mālukyaputta were markedly different. Bāhiya of the bark-cloth was the Buddha's foremost disciple of quick understanding. Mālukyaputta, on the other hand, was an elderly monk of slower faculties. Despite his age he had neglected to apply himself to meditation. Perhaps it was a belated sense of urgency that moved him to ask the Buddha for "instruction in brief."

Whereas Bāhiya gained enlightenment the instant he heard the Buddha's words, Mālukyaputta had to practice ardently before attaining awakening. The difference in ability between the disciples suggests the teaching is suitable for a wide range of temperaments. Although Bāhiya's tale is more glamorous, most of us resemble Mālukyaputta, so we must make the effort to practice.

Many people say, "I don't have enough concentration to meditate." But vipassanā requires only momentary concentration, which anyone can develop. Like medicine, meditation is not something for which one needs an aptitude, but a prescription for illness—the illness called "delusion."

Vipassanā, Mahāsi Sayādaw tells us, begins only when we observe the activity of the six senses. Why six senses rather than five? In Buddhism the mind is considered the sixth sense-organ, and mental impressions a type of sense-data. Insight meditation is a technique of noticing the sights, sounds, smells, tastes, touches and mental events of moment-to-moment experience. When applied systematically this practice leads to wisdom—the wisdom that dispels the false belief in a permanent self.

To understand the Bāhiya teaching—and vipassanā itself—one should be familiar with the Buddhist distinction between conventional and ultimate truth. These truths can be regarded as two ways of looking at the same phenomenal world. As an example I talk about viewing a pointillist painting from two perspectives. This is, of course, only a metaphor. I don't mean to suggest ultimate realities are literally atomic dots.

What does it mean to "Just See"? As Mahāsi Sayādaw explains, "Only bare attention is to be paid to what arises at one or the other of the six sense doors." In the case of seeing this means to note the instant that eye and image make contact, before the mind alters the experience by describing or judging it. When looking at an image with bare attention the meditator becomes a disinterested observer. Brushing aside subjective desires, associations and feelings, he regards the form objectively, as if seeing it for the first time. (Some call this "beginner's mind.") The same applies to the experience of hearing, smelling, tasting, touching and even thinking.

But as most meditators know, this is easier said than done. That's because mindfulness and insight are not yet strong enough. The solution is to begin by focusing mainly on sensations of touch. Tactility, the most distinct of the senses, is experienced as motion, pressure, or temperature. Mahāsi Sayādaw recommends observing motion by noting the expanding and contracting movements of the abdomen that occur in respiration. (Instructions for this meditation exercise are given in Appendix Two.)

However, as Nyanaponika Thera points out, "Bare attention can generally be maintained only during a limited time of ordinary life, apart from periods expressly given to its application." (*The Heart of Buddhist Meditation*, p. 49). Fortunately, we don't have to Just See, Hear and Know all day long to progress in meditation. When engaged in activities of daily life that require abstract thinking, we can use general mindfulness and clear comprehension to be more aware of our actions, thoughts and intentions. But *some* time should be devoted to formal meditation—even if only thirty minutes per day—if we want to make a permanent end of suffering. And even in the midst of complex activities, there are moments here and there that can be noted with bare attention—moments, for instance, of changing posture, waiting in line at a store, hearing a dog bark, taking a drink, touching a doorknob, and so on. All day long rudimentary perceptions alternate with more complex ones. Through the practice of vipassanā those throwaway moments become useful—each one a step along the path.

The teaching that I call "Just Seeing" can be understood on at least two levels: that of personal meditative experience (by far the most important), and the microscopic level of reality described in Buddhist metaphysics (*Abhidhamma*), consisting of a stream of continually changing mental and physical phenomena, inconceivably fleeting. Whereas the main text of this book deals chiefly with the former, Appendix One looks at the moment-to-moment process of perception. An examination on this micro-scale helps to clarify the method and purpose of insight meditation. The resulting knowledge can give the student increased confidence in vipassanā practice.

For narrative simplicity I often refer only to seeing, without reference to the other senses. This is not meant to suggest that seeing is superior to or qualitatively different from hearing, touching, and so on. All sense-impressions have equal value as working-grounds for insight. But it bears repeating that during meditation we focus mostly on tactile impressions, since those are the easiest to watch.

Ordinary language has been used wherever possible in order to make these teachings accessible to beginners as well as experienced meditators.

At this point it will be useful to give a brief synopsis of each of the chapters in this book: Chapter One discusses the nature of observation, the two types of meditation, and the power of sense-impressions to trigger desire. Chapter Two spells out the difference between ultimate and conventional reality. Chapter Three describes the process of perception and defines "Just Seeing" in more detail, as well as describing the actual experience. It also looks at the difference between Just Seeing and the pre-verbal perceptions of an infant. Chapter Four describes the two types of mindfulness and explains why Just Seeing cannot result in immoral behavior. The Buddhist term "nonself" is discussed, as well as the need to move flexibly between ultimate and conventional reality. Chapter Five touches on the deceptive nature of ordinary perception and the benefits of Just Seeing. Chapter Six describes the sixteen stages of insight-knowledge, explains the difference between mindfulness, wise attention and clear comprehension, and gives some guidelines on meditation practice. Chapter Seven discusses nonattachment and the way in which our perspective changes when reality is viewed from the ultimate standpoint. Appendix One, in addition to unraveling the perceptual process, offers an interpretation of the phrase "just think" in terms of the Abhidhamma. Readers who wish to begin meditating right away can go straight to the practice instructions in Appendix Two.

The Buddhist path can be summarized as the practice of morality, concentration and wisdom. Although this book emphasizes the last aspect, the other two are essential components of liberation. In order to benefit from meditation one must avoid intentionally harming others and oneself. As a minimum standard of morality, the Buddha taught his disciples to refrain from the following: 1) killing (including insects) 2) stealing 3) sexual misconduct 4) lying and harsh speech, and 5) drinking alcohol and· taking recreational drugs. These are called the "Five Precepts." What about concentration? It is developed alongside mindfulness and wisdom during the practice of insight meditation.

A number of interpretations of the Bāhiya teaching exist. This book follows the Theravadan tradition, with an emphasis on the teachings of Mahāsi Sayādaw. However, it is well to remember the Buddha's caution against dogmatic adherence to any view. In the end the true proving-ground is our direct experience of realities here and now, in the present moment.

The purpose of this book is not only to explore the Buddhist teachings, but also to encourage the reader to practice meditation. Just Seeing, according to Mahāsi Sayādaw, is an event that occurs when mindfulness and insight are fairly developed, but it is something all meditators can eventually experience. Anyone seeking an end to suffering (i.e., all of us) should be heartened by these words: "Nibbāna," the Sayādaw wrote, "is within easy reach of everyone who practices insight meditation."

Cynthia Thatcher
January, 2008
Denver, Colorado

CHAPTER 1

Elements fly together from all corners, only to land as a spontaneous composition, impossible to anticipate, called the present moment. Right now, for instance, some pieces are coming together: hammer and nails, a wall, the scent of jasmine rising from a teapot, a friend's gift of a large art print (framed and lying on the floor), and ourselves, who've just begun to hang the picture.

Though it's heavier than it looks, we manage to hoist the print, to brace the mass of wood and glass against the wall and, with a light scraping sound, slide it down until the hanging-wire catches on the nail. After straightening the frame, we stand back to observe.

The painting is Georges Seurat's *A Sunday Afternoon on the Island of La Grande Jatte*, his famous scene of Parisians enjoying a waterside park. On a wide lawn beside the river Seine (and its boats) we see people lounging in the grass or walking among the trees. With the painting's long shadows and golden light the mood is serene–the stillness of a leisurely summer afternoon.

But as the eye darts from trees to people to boats, we wonder if we're missing something. After all, we're not expert in the visual arts. How should we interpret these colored shapes? Painters learn to see in a skillful way, to find in line, color and perspective the secrets of their leverage. We need an artist's eye—then we could crack the visual code.

Unintentionally, we've hung the French master's print opposite the image of a greater Master: a picture of the Buddha—of his statue, rather—at Sri Lanka's Jayanthi Vihāra. Instead of a blank wall the Buddha's gaze will now fall upon the French trees.

All the while conditions keep shifting. Here and there a grain falls, enough to tip the scale the other way. Catching sight of the Buddha's face, we imagine his gaze throws a ray of knowledge into the hall, an almost palpable beam, and under it the artistic concerns scatter.

Never mind cracking the visual code. Why set our sights too low? A new train of thought begins to form. What if we could learn to see in such a way as to crack the shell of ignorance itself, as the

Buddha taught his disciples to do? And by so doing, become free of all unease? For the Buddha discovered a link between a way of seeing and happiness itself. "What," we ask ourselves, "would the *Buddha* have seen, looking at Seurat's painting?" More than that, how can we see forms as he would have, with the eye of wisdom? Suddenly this is the compelling question.

Yes—but how to answer it? The hallway blurs away as the mind turns instead toward the corridors of memory, looking down one passage after another in search of a relevant phrase. The scent of rain drifts in through the window; we hear the *Pok! Pok!* as drops strike the flag-stones, and these words flash in the mind: "Here, O bhikkhus, a bhikkhu knows the eye and material forms and the fetter that arises dependent on both" (*Majjhima Nikāya* 10). It's a phrase from the suttas, a phrase which could serve as our starting-point.

Seeing is usually regarded as a seamless event, but this passage tells us to break the process into its components: one, the eye itself; two, images, the colored shapes the eye sees; and three, those mental states that bubble to life when eye and image intersect. Our task is to know these components, to observe them so as to understand their nature.

But don't we already know it's good to be aware of what we see? Is there anything new in such an instruction? After all, the Buddha wasn't unique in touting the value of observation. Thinkers and artists through the ages have said that observation leads to knowledge. "Use your eyes," the saying goes. Being observant can also bring an appreciation of the beauty around us. "Observe," da Vinci said, "in the streets at twilight, when the day is cloudy, the loveliness and tenderness spread on the faces of men and women." Then there are those fictional sleuths whose *tours de force* in observation astound us: the likes of Sherlock Holmes who, merely by looking at a horseshoe, can tell the weight and breed of the horse it belonged to.

And yet those feats of observation, while impressive, only extend what we do every day. If we didn't already notice and interpret differences of shape and color, how would we know a certain moving speck was a pigeon, say, not a plane or a kite? Knowing a pigeon depends on conceptualization. By means of thinking, the mind leaps from seeing an unnamed color-patch to perceiving a bird.

And so, quite able to tell a plane from a pigeon, we muddle through. Yet we tend to notice only what fits the elaborate network of our own desires, letting the rest blur into the twilight. Most of us would admit to the presence of black holes in our awareness. Into these gaps fall many things—some trivial, some not: the location of our keys, the pattern of the kitchen floor, the color of someone's eyes, the presence of *dukkha* (unsatisfactoriness).

While almost everyone would agree it's good to be attentive, the reasons for valuing observation differ. The artist observes for the sake of beauty; the detective, to gain the evidence to solve a crime. But the primary reason to observe our experience, the Buddha taught, isn't to alleviate boredom, find the keys, accrue beauty, or solve a case. It is to liberate the mind from dukkha. An undercurrent of dissatisfaction runs through our lives for which mindfulness is the only antidote.[1] We need to be observant in order to free ourselves from every ill, including the anxiety that always seems to flicker at the edge of the mind.

In order to be free of suffering we must identify suffering's cause. Observation isn't an end in itself—and yet without it, how could we find the source of the fire that burns us? Seeing the fire, we can put it out.

But what should we observe? Only ourselves. The whole universe, the Buddha said, is contained in this fathom-long body with its perceiving mind. By skillfully observing our own minds and bodies we can arrive at the deepest nature of reality, the universal characteristics of *all* phenomena. That insight will stop the cycle of suffering.

Detectives, scientists, and others skilled in observation may pay great attention to what they see and hear, and yet largely ignore their response to those impressions. But the Buddha taught beings to observe their response very closely, from moment to moment. This is key because in truth suffering and happiness are generated in the mind's reaction, not from the sights and sounds themselves. If we understand this we can be happy even when experiencing unpleasant sense-impressions.

---

1.   Mindfulness, the Buddha taught, is the only way to permanent freedom from suffering, Nibbāna. The entire Noble Eightfold Path entails morality, concentration and wisdom. See: p. 5, footnote 3.

And what about the *type* of observation the Buddha taught? It, too, differs from what we're used to, and the difference runs deep. In the Buddhist teachings we learn that genuine knowing differs from verbalization and conceptual understanding. The knowledge that frees one from suffering has nothing to do with thinking. Described in Pali as *cakkhu*, vision, it is a type of knowing that sees reality directly, in a visual epiphany or insight, as clearly as seeing your hand with your eyes. And yet it's seen by the mind.

We said before that observing a colored shape, so as to know if it's a pigeon or a plane, requires conceptualization. All day long we narrate and describe our experience, although this inner commentary is so elusive and quick, we're often unaware of it. But what would it be like to experience reality as it is, without a tinge of descriptive overlay? The Buddha taught a species of awareness that leads to just that; it's a knowing that undercuts the inner narration on every level. The beam of this awareness can be turned onto any facet of experience, including the root of cognition itself. Those very mental formations by which we leap from a colored speck to a pigeon become, in themselves, objects to observe.

Although conceptual knowledge is invaluable in its sphere, it is inadequate for penetrating ultimate truth. As long as we cling to the judgments of the intellect, the features of ultimate truth remain obscured. (Yet it isn't conventional knowledge itself, but the *attachment* to it that can become an obstacle.)

It's a radical idea—that in order to reach the truth we don't have to pile up more thoughts but only part the mental clouds long enough to glimpse what is already fully-formed. Instead of gathering more conceptual knowledge, we sweep the mind clear with the tool of continuous attention. Illumination is immediate when we cease adding levels of distortion to what is directly before us. The Four Noble Truths,[2] the Buddha declared, are already manifest, arrayed around and "through" the mind.

Anyone can learn to observe his experience free (for a time) of

2. The Four Noble Truths, or *ariya sacca*, are: 1) the truth of *dukkha*—that all existence is unsatisfactory because unstable and liable to suffering; 2) the origin of *dukkha*, which is craving; 3) the extinguishing of *dukkha*, which is *nirodha* or realization of Nibbāna; and 4) the Noble Eightfold Path which leads to that extinguishing.

the screens of verbal description, thereby seeing reality as it is. In seeing this clearly one is freed of all distress. The training required is the practice of vipassanā meditation, as part of the Noble Eightfold Path.[3]

Vipassanā—meaning insight—differs from meditation techniques based solely on concentration. The aim of vipassanā or insight meditation is to see reality as it is, whereas the aim of concentration (samatha) is to make the mind tranquil, temporarily suppressing mental impurities. Vipassanā is sometimes referred to as "mindfulness" meditation. To be sure, some concentration is necessary for mindfulness work, but not the high degree needed for the meditative absorptions.

In pure concentration one fixes awareness on a single object and keeps it there. In vipassanā, on the other hand, one observes the ever-changing phenomena occurring in one's own body and mind. The aim isn't stillness or temporary bliss, but wisdom. With wisdom comes release from distress and hurt—permanent release from dukkha.

To practice vipassanā is to be aware of the present moment to the *nth* degree—now after now after now. By observing sights, sounds, smells, tastes, touches, motions, emotions and thoughts as soon as they are sensed we know them just as they are, distinct from the names and ideas *about* them. The mindfulness that leads to wisdom isn't just an extra helping of normal attention but a special kind of awareness, part of a broad strategy that spins the tables of perspective one-hundred-eighty degrees.

Now our thoughts have wandered far from Seurat's painting. Yet even as we notice this, the blue, green and ochre patches rush back into place—a jigsaw puzzle coming together as we watch. Here again are the trees, the sailboats, the men gazing at the river, the women sitting in the grass.

The Buddha said that we should know the eye and image, and those fetters that arise when eye and image touch. Why list these things separately? Why not just say, "Know all the aspects of

---

3. The complete Pali term for "insight meditation" is "vipassanā bhāvanā." The Eightfold Path to eliminate suffering consists of: right speech, right action, right livelihood, right effort, right mindfulness, right concentration, right view and right thought.

seeing"? Because in truth they are separate things. When they are knotted together we can't know the true nature of each component. By untangling the knot and separating the strands, however, we'll find that each condition requires the others if seeing is to happen. As we begin to understand that seeing is a matter of impersonal conditions striking together, that among those conditions is nothing called a "self," we won't assume, "[The body's] eyes are *our* eyes, the sights they see are things *we* see, the sensation of seeing is something *we* sense."[4]

Before us now is an image—Seurat's painting. The blind patches of paint on the canvas don't know, themselves, if they're azure or scarlet, or whether they're meant to be sky or lake, a woman's lips or the blood of Christ. A perceiver is required if they're to be known. But when perceiving them, what do we see?

Most of the time we don't experience pure color-patches. Instead we tend to "see" in terms of named Things. On the right side of Seurat's painting, for example, are some colored shapes that we easily recognize as a well-dressed couple. The woman, wearing a plum-colored skirt, holds an umbrella in one hand and a leash (tethered to a monkey) in the other. At her feet we see a small brown dog leaping toward a bigger dog. In the left foreground a workman with a pipe reclines in the grass, while another man, with a top hat and cane, gazes toward the water. There's a matron mending, a little girl skipping, and another girl holding a posy of flowers. We see a group of trees in the background on the right, and the Seine, with its many boats, on the left.

Notice what happens when we "see" in this manner: As soon as the eye scans the picture each swatch of color raises a name, its flagpole of identity: *tree, boat, dog, top hat, woman, umbrella, skirt.* We're aware of these concepts the instant we perceive the aqua and ocher shapes (just as we instantly recognize a colored speck as a pigeon).

The mind unconsciously compares these names to remembered things of the same names, and before we know it the color-patches of the present are imbued with associations from the past. Memory and imagination take over. Here is only paper tinted with ink and yet, as imagination strikes the image we seem to feel

---

4. Kor Khao Suan Luang, *Reading the Mind*, p. 24.

the sailboats dip and bob, the lawn brush against our palms, prickly and cool. We sense the weight of sunlight on upturned faces.

A chain reaction is set off as each round of labels triggers another, more elaborate, one. In the twinkling of an eye liking and disliking get into the act. Along with the names spring valuations: "I like the sailboat—but not the plum dress."

Outside, the rain has stopped. As we turn toward the window, reaching for the teacup on the sill, a new sight swings into view: the evening clouds above the mountains in the west. It's another picture, one framed by the window this time, and we admire its loveliness.

But as the mind drifts, caught on a tide of attraction, other images rise up from memory, unasked-for: the face of a loved one; sunlight falling through a white curtain; an abandoned lot overrun with wildflowers. If a painting, being only a representation, can draw from us cords of feeling, how much more are we moved by these "real" images? Delight springs up when we see pleasant forms—delight, and desire.

Why does desire arise whenever the eye touches something lovely? Because the sight causes a pleasant feeling, which we want to prolong. But here's the problem: we assume that if the image can be obtained it will keep on generating the feeling of delight. Believing the contact and pleasure of seeing to be stable, the mind latches on to the image, trying to snare it in a web of attachment. But in truth the pleasant feeling can't be made to last. The English phrase "catch your eye" is apt. As image and pleasure slip away it's the weaver who's caught in a web of wanting.

Other emotions may arise when hue and eye intersect. Suppose the shape called "spouse's face" comes into view. The mouth, as you watch, curves upward in a smile, and your heart and mind grow light. But when the image alters, your mood mirrors the change. The face turns red, the eyebrows draw together, and as the smile reverses, so does your happiness.

Or suppose you look at your own face in the mirror. In truth you see only a patch of color, not an "I." When you're younger, the sight may please you. But later, if you spot creases, or loose skin under the chin, or white threads running through the hair, you think "old" and "unattractive." Disliking the image, you feel distressed. Why? Because you've tied it to a concept called "self." (But you're not disturbed by an elderly stranger's face—that image has nothing to do with your self).

We begin to sense the causal pattern, begin to see that emotions, from joy to depression, can be whisked up in an instant when the right colored shape touches the eye. And among those emotions are the fetters—craving, envy, hatred, and other unskillful mental states.

The fetters that appear due to contact with sense-impressions resemble an array of ropes—mental ones—that tie beings to suffering, to the ongoing stream of sensation. Although ten in all,[5] the fetters are rooted in the following mental pollutants: 1) greed (*lobha*), 2) hatred (*dosa*), and 3) delusion (*moha*). If someone can eliminate these three, he'll automatically destroy the ten fetters.

All of our reactions to sights could be classed as one of the following: liking, disliking, or indifference. Liking could be called the top of a plant whose root is greed, or desire. Disliking, on the other hand, is rooted in hatred. Although liking and disliking are milder states, greed and hatred are the origins from which they spring. When an object is provocative enough, the emotions flare out with corresponding intensity. Greed and hatred, the Buddhist teachings tell us, are mental factors always dormant in the ordinary mind, factors triggered into action by an appropriate object.[6]

What if neither liking nor disliking arises? Though indifferent to the image, we might still be viewing it through the mist of ignorance. Attraction, aversion and deluded indifference cloud the mind, warping our view of the world around (and within) us. If we could burn off the haze, mind and matter would appear as they actually are. But how to burn it off? The first step is simply to observe the mind as it reacts to sights, sounds, and other sense-impressions:

---

5. The ten fetters are: sensual craving, ill-will, conceit, wrong views, doubt, attachment to rituals, existential craving, envy, stinginess and ignorance.
6. The fifty-two mental factors (*cetasika*) include morally neutral phenomena such as volition, feeling and attention, as well as wholesome or unwholesome factors like compassion, mindfulness, greed, and delusion.

There is indeed a method, monks, by following which a monk … could affirm insight … And what is that method? Herein, monks, a monk, seeing an object with the eye, either recognizes within him the existence of lust [desire], aversion or ignorance, thus: 'I have lust, aversion or ignorance,' or recognizes the non-existence of these qualities within him, thus: 'I have not lust, aversion, or ignorance.'[7] (SN 35:152)

Rather than trying to suppress desire, hatred and delusion, we can undermine their power by applying constant attention. If we're aware of those impurities early enough, they disappear as soon as they're sensed. If they don't arise we're aware of that, too, simply knowing they're absent at that moment.

But catching these things is an ongoing proposition. Since images keep pouring in through the eye, desire and aversion keep foaming on up. Whether we're looking, for example, at a painting, a burned-out building, or the evening lights reflected on a river, the pictures affect us. And it's not only sights; sounds, smells, tastes, touches and mental phenomena keep bombarding us, too.

The Buddha urged us to notice how much the mind wobbles when the eye contacts color, how reliably an attractive image bends our consciousness toward it. But when faced with an unpleasant sight—an angry face, for instance—the mind tries to swerve away.

Liking and disliking swing the mind between them like a tethered ball. We let the body rest, but even in dreams the mind is chasing or running from objects, unable to stop and be still. These pendulum swings can happen from one moment to the next. During all this oscillation some of our autonomy dribbles out.

As much as we dislike being controlled by others, rarely do we notice the insidious power of images. The more we observe the connection between the scenes prodding the eye and the emotions that trouble the heart, the more it will be seen how much freedom we forfeit to sights. Keeping track, even for a day, of how many times your gaze is unconsciously reeled toward pleasing shapes is—pardon the pun—an eye-opening exercise. In a crowded street all eyes swivel toward a beautiful face. We look up to see the new moon, down to watch a sparrow drinking from a pool. It's surprising what

---

7. "Ignorance" does not refer to lack of education, but failure to realize the Four Noble Truths.

might snare the eye—even a bare twig gilded by an angle of light. How often, though, do we stop to look at a rusted can or a brick wall? That's not to say it's better to look at a wall than a pretty face. There's nothing wrong with looking at anything. It's our attachment and lack of awareness that are troubling. If we don't see how much freedom of mind has been sacrificed, how can we begin to reclaim it?

If we could rewind time and meet the Great Masters of art, perhaps they would admit that despite their control over beauty on the canvas, beauty still mastered their hearts—because skill at manipulating visual form doesn't make one its sovereign, or immune to its influence. Most likely those painters were just as overcome by color and visual form as are the rest of us, whose common predicament the Buddha described:

> Herein, friends, a monk, seeing an object with the eye, feels attachment for objects that charm, feels aversion from objects that displease, abides without having established mindfulness of the body ... He realizes not, in its true nature, that emancipation of heart, that emancipation of wisdom ... So dwelling, friends, [visible] objects overcome a monk, a monk overcomes not objects. (Ibid., 35:202)

But what, it might be asked, accounts for the emotional force of anything we see? Where does it reside? In the object itself, the eye, or somewhere else? Two of the Buddha's disciples addressed this question:

> 'Suppose, friend, two oxen, one white and one black, tied by one rope or one yoke-tie. Would one be right in saying that the black ox is the bond for the white one, or that the white one is the bond for the black one?' 'No, friend. It is not so.' 'But the rope or the yoke-tie which binds the two—that is the bond that unites them. So it is with the eye and objects ... It is the desire and lust which arise owing to them that form the bond that unites them.' (Ibid., 35:191)

Because we habitually cling to the pleasant and resist the unpleasant, sights have been overcoming us for the whole of our lives. When the object is pleasant we don't mind being overcome. But when our happiness depends on conditions that cannot be manipulated, how can we hope to be free of distress? What replaces the joy when the lovely shape changes?

While never denying the pleasure to be found in beautiful objects, the Buddha pointed out that pleasure is not the unalloyed happiness we imagine. Pleasure, being ephemeral, is twisted through with disappointment. "Where joy most revels," Shakespeare wrote, "grief doth most lament".

How can we find happiness in something that changes, without also finding distress? The Buddha said: "Devas (heavenly beings) and mankind, monks, delight in objects, they are excited by objects. It is owing to this instability, the coming to an end, the ceasing of objects, monks, that devas and mankind live woefully" (ibid., 35:136).

The desire to experience pleasant sights and sounds may lead to conflict with those closest to us. "When sense-pleasures are the cause," the Buddha said, "a mother disputes with her son, a son disputes with his mother ... a brother disputes with a brother ... a friend disputes with a friend". One is reminded of the wake of suffering left by the legendary beauty Helen of Troy, whose apt nickname was Lady of Sorrows.

As a result of wanting to acquire beautiful forms, we might find ourselves disputing with strangers, too. Perhaps the store didn't have the flowers we wanted, or the right color paint. Someone damaged the car or ruined a rug. The handyman muffed the job. The hairstylist gave a bad cut. Due to desire we scald others with words, become depressed; or else the inflamed mind, thinking, "I should have chosen the *other* blouse, or carpet, or house," becomes trapped in a wheel of regret or worry.

When looking at a wall or some other neutral sight, which sparks neither desire nor aversion, a more subtle response occurs: the misperception of the visual form, whereby we take what is only a momentary flash of color for a persisting thing. Although we regard oil paintings, for example, as relatively stable objects and things like sunsets as ephemeral, any image becomes transitory when it falls into the moving current of awareness.

A painting, in its conventional sense as an enduring object "out there", is not identical with the tingle of color experienced when seeing it. The viewer says, "I'm looking at Seurat's painting." But the image that touches our awareness is just a momentary part of the ever-moving movie reeling past the eyes—as are any of the shapes we behold through the visual organ. Though we regard some images as persisting Things that can be returned to whenever we wish, our *experience* of those forms isn't stable. Objects can only be know as part of the continuous stream of perception, our personal movie.

As we turn away from Seurat's painting and look toward the window again, the moving screen of perception presents another scene to the eye: a few poplar trees, a field of oatgrass, the broken line of the mountains. From the perspective of the internal movie, the image of the painting ceases to exist as soon as we stop seeing it. Conventionally speaking, the piece of matter—the wood and tinted paper—may or may not remain, but the particular instance of color that happens when light strikes the retina just so is gone. Those frames of the movie are in the past.

We read in *The Path of Purification*:

> Just as there is no store, prior to its arising, of the sound that arises when a lute is played, nor does it persist as a store when it has ceased, but on the contrary, not having been, it is brought into being owing to the lute and the man's appropriate effort, and having been, it vanishes—so too all material and immaterial states, not having been are brought into being, having been, they vanish. (Buddhaghosa, XX, 96)

Although we can remember Seurat's painting while looking out the window, recollecting is not seeing. While recalling the painting we're actually *seeing* something else.[8] We can only view one thing at a time, and that from within the closed circle of perception we can't jump out of. Although we can be reasonably sure of many things, what can we know with genuine certainty—know, that is, without doubt?

Whether the mannequins spring to life after we leave the store or it all sputters back to the void as soon as our attention swings away, we can only know the next thing onto which our small light falls. Whatever that awareness touches as it roams through the world it illumines momentarily and so, for us, renders *momentary*. Even when looking at the painting we don't take in the whole

---

8. In the strict sense, however, we cannot see or hear when remembering. Consciousness can only know one thing at a time.

picture at once. The eye perceives one piece at a time like the blind men grasping different parts of an elephant. The gaze darts from the woman's skirt to her face to the shadow her head makes, as memory splices the images into a single frame.

Since a movie is always *moving*, we can't stop the perceptual show, can't pause the inner film to grab a few good parts we want to pocket. Still, we try. Yet in fact whatever is grasped at dissolves even as we reach for it. Lacking insight-knowledge[9] we can't see the dissolve, can't perceive the moment-to-moment disintegration of our world, though it goes on regardless.

This daily spate of unpainted images—where is the Great Master who is able to master *them*? They rise and set on their own schedule, and if the face of a loved one moves us more than does a portrait, or the autumn light falling through red and gold leaves affects us more than does its painted counterpart, doesn't it also cause more distress when it changes? And change it must (there's the rub).

In time one might learn to understand Seurat's painting, and other great works, with an artist's eye. But to what end, when we have yet to understand, in the ultimate sense, the visual stream of everyday experience? After all, it's this daily flow of forms we most need to comprehend. Not to obtain knowledge for its own sake, but in order to free the mind from dukkha.

The usual strategy, in the search for happiness, is to seek out as many beautiful sense-stimuli as possible while fervently trying to avoid unpleasant and neutral ones. As the architect Ernest Gimson wrote, "Life is commensurate with the number of beautiful impressions that can be squeezed into it. Let us have as many as we can." This approach, which focuses entirely on the objects being perceived while ignoring the perceiving mind, is understandable but misguided. It shows one does not yet know where true happiness comes from, or how suffering arises. Although it is fine to enjoy the good things of life in moderation (provided we don't cling to them or hurt anyone in the process), in reaching for the unrealistic goal of *continual* pleasure and beauty we ultimately exhaust ourselves trying to twist things, people and events into whatever pattern is our current ideal. And along the way we generate enormous agitation in

---

9. The insight into the impermanence, unsatisfactoriness and impersonality of mind and matter, developed through vipassanā meditation.

the mind, which, ironically, is far more unpleasant than seeing an ugly sight or hearing a harsh sound.

Instead of trying to manipulate an intractable stream of phenomena, what if we swung our attention around? Couldn't we master our own minds, if not the fickle conditions of the outside world? Lasting happiness, the Buddha declared, comes from the mind, not from outside. We can still participate actively in life, yet by training awareness on the mind itself as it responds to the ongoing barrage of sensation we will find release from all distress, including the subtle anxiety that underlies even the happiest hours. At the same time, in purifying the mind of those mental factors that cause suffering, we protect and inspire others.

What prevents us from finding lasting happiness? For one thing, the doubt that anything better exists. "The untaught manyfolk, monks, know of no refuge from painful feeling save sensual pleasure" (SN 36:6). Having nothing to compare with pain except a momentary, sensual comfort, we don't see the value of nonattachment. Regarding pleasure and pain as opposites that have no common characteristic, we fail to see that pleasure is unsatisfactory, too.

Imagine viewing a color chart that shows different shades of a blue pigment. On the extreme left is the palest robin's egg, almost white. At the other end is the darkest navy, a hair's breadth away from black. Although the navy appears so different from the robin's egg, the two colors are in essence the same—only different saturations of the same hue. All the tints on the chart have the same pigment in common. As different as they are, none could be called red or yellow. You could move as far to the right or the left of the chart as you liked, but you'd never escape the attribute of blue. Likewise, pleasure and pain, happiness and misery, are merely different shades in the same spectrum of suffering.

"Suffering" here means dukkha, which refers to the instability of all conditioned phenomena, the impermanence that renders even the most delightful moments ultimately unsatisfactory. The Buddha, a friend to all beings, was forever calling, Over here! urging them to come and see the element called Nibbāna. Nibbāna, which he declared the highest bliss, refers to the complete cessation of dukkha. It is said to be a kind of happiness superior to what we know, that can't be compared to what we know. And it doesn't change.

CHAPTER 2

As part of the path leading to Nibbāna, the Buddha prescribed a specific technique for seeing: *When seeing, just see.* One stops at the mere sensation of seeing; the mind adds nothing more. Instead of viewing things through rose or dark glasses, one knows phenomena just as they are—without describing, verbalizing, liking or disliking them.

But for most of us, more is required than a four-word formula. Exactly how does one Just See? To begin with, we'll need a visible object. And why not Seurat's painting, since it's still in front of us? Any object can become kindling for wisdom's fire. Yet we won't regard the picture in terms of artistic merit or even as an *objet d'art*, but only as the visible datum it fundamentally is. Just Seeing demands a democratic gaze.

Moving closer to the painting now, we focus on the largest tree. But in a moment the mind stops short. What we have here isn't the usual painted tree. Something's missing.

Here are no seamless bands of color, no blended patches of tint as seen in other paintings. The linden is made up of countless specks—the whole tree including the trunk—a smattering of separate blue, yellow and red dots. Continuing to examine the picture inch by inch, we find that the boats on the water, the people on the lawn, their faces and clothes—all are a sprinkling of motes, as if the canvas had been caught out in a rain of paint.

Curious. (We remember, now, Seurat was a pointillist.) Odder still, when focusing on the individual specks it's like viewing a different painting from the one we hung on the wall just minutes ago with its placid lawn, people and boats. From this new perspective, beings and objects have vanished. The eye sees an empty landscape. The sense of time is gone, along with the languid June atmosphere. The Seine, the trees, the monkey's face—all have exploded into particles, scattered across space.

And yet it should come as no surprise that things are not as they seem. Even according to ordinary knowledge (remember your eighth grade science class?), the everyday objects that we take to be stable and motionless—including the slab of canvas and pigment called a "painting"—resemble clouds of whirling midges with more empty space than mass. Nor should we be surprised to learn that those who look, with clear comprehension, into the surface of their own experience might stumble onto other gaps—faults in the continuity, openings in the ordinary world. Passing across an invisible threshold one abandons the familiar landscape of objects and people. The mind enters a terrain of impersonal phenomena where identity can't happen and stability is exposed as a misperception, a perceptual sleight-of-hand. This primary reality is called, in Buddhism, *paramattha-sacca*, meaning ultimate truth.[10]

What is ultimate truth? In Buddhist philosophy, ultimate realities are the raw mental and material phenomena of existence, which can't be further reduced. Out of these genuine but momentary building blocks the mind fashions concepts, the objects of the conventional realm such as sailboats and trees. Because they are compounds that can be taken apart, such formations don't exist as things-in-themselves. A sailboat is broken down into mast, hull, rudder; a tree dissected into trunk, branch, root; but ultimate realities are indivisible.

Stepping back from the painting, boats and trees come into being as the eye "pulls" the specks together, like scattered fish drawn up in a net. But the suggestion of cohesion and identity is only the mind's fabrication, an illusion of perspective that doesn't alter the fundamental discreteness of the dots.

The trees, sailboats, and lawns in the picture all boil down to one kind of thing. So, too, the varied shapes of the everyday world that multiply like cells, the new varieties that pile up like clouds, the countless hybrids of thought and form, all come down to the two components of ultimate truth: *nāma* and *rūpa*.[11]

"Nāma" means mind, "rūpa," matter. The mind is formless, intangible, but matter has form. In the limitless circle of the

10. We are referring to conditioned ultimate realities, i.e., *citta, cetasika* and *rūpa*, not Nibbāna, which is unchanging and permanent. See next footnote.
11. Strictly speaking, there are four ultimate realities: citta (consciousness), cetasika (mental factors), rūpa (matter) and Nibbāna. Since ordinary meditators cannot perceive consciousness apart from its mental factors, in vipassanā we speak of citta and cetasika together as nāma, mind.

universe are found only these two things, mind and matter. (Nibbāna also exists, but it is supramundane. Still, it can be seen by those living in the mundane world.)

In vipassanā meditation, "rūpa" refers to bare sense-impressions: color, sound, flavor, scent and touches. ("Touches" indicate the characteristics of hardness and temperature. Hardness or softness, heat or coolness, are known through the tactile sense.[12]) We may not think of them as such, but sense-impressions are a type of materiality. They are, in fact, our only direct experience of the latter.

Rūpa is not conscious. Sound cannot hear; color cannot see. Material phenomena must be touched by a mind in order to be experienced, so we speak of nāma-rūpa. "Nāma-rūpa" means "mind-and-matter" or "mind-and-form."

Nāma and rūpa serve two functions in our moment-to-moment experience. One is the function of knowing. Nāma, the mind, performs that job. Another is the function of being known. The thing being known is called the "object."

An object is anything of which the mind is aware. It does not have to be material. It can be either rūpa or nāma, corporeal or incorporeal.[13] But the knower, the faculty aware of an object, is always nāma, mind. Simply put: rūpas are known. Nāmas know (rūpas and other nāmas).

Mind and object come together in each moment. Whenever they make contact, experience happens. For example, sound vibrations are rūpa; the mind is the faculty that perceives the sound. The fragrance given off by an oil is rūpa; the mind perceives the scent. Color is rūpa; nāma, the mind, *cognizes* color. Each moment of experience contains one knower and one object (but the knower is not an ego. It is impersonal, nonself). Units of mind and object collide and dissolve, collide and dissolve, producing existence from moment to moment.

Objects are not conscious; they lack awareness. Rūpas are

---

12. Touches or tangible phenomena include bodily motion, since it is perceived through the tactile sense.
13. "Object" (*ārammaṇa*) refers to the six phenomena of which we have direct experience: visible form, sound, scent, taste, tangibles and mental objects.

always objects, not knowers; but not all objects are rūpas. As we said, mental phenomena such as thoughts, emotions, and feelings can also function as objects. In that case, one nāma serves as the object known *by* another nāma. Having two nāmas may seem confusing, as if there would be two knowers. But only one nāma at a time can be the knower.[14]

Observing nāma and rūpa isn't as hard as it sounds. Ultimate reality is the undeniable part of experience. Although people might debate the artistic worth of Seurat's painting, who would deny that when looking at it one sees color? Although the word "ultimate" suggests something on a high shelf out of reach, paramattha dhammas are not distant or unattainable. Ultimate truth is simply the natural state of things, far simpler to handle, in fact, than the conventional, because it consists of only two components.

Conventional truth (*sammuti-sacca*), on the other hand, refers to conceptual objects such as a tree, boat or person, as well as to the names of things. Unlike ultimate realities, concepts and names can proliferate endlessly.

The Thai vipassanā teacher Achan Sobin Namto uses the example of sound to explain the difference between conventional and ultimate reality: Most cultures have a word for the object called "bell" in English. The French say "cloche," the Thai, "rakang." These words are relative, conventional truth, changing from person to person, but the sound (rūpa) you hear when striking the bell is ultimate truth. Disagreements can arise when dealing with conventional reality. Someone says, "I hear a bell." Someone else says, "No, I hear a cloche." Yet in the ultimate sense we hear neither. A bell does not enter the ear. Neither does a cloche. We

---

14. For example, suppose one moment of consciousness—let's call it A— observes a sound (a type of rūpa). After observing the sound, consciousness A dies out. In the next moment a new blip of consciousness arises, B. Let's suppose B observes A, the previous moment of consciousness. The thing observed by consciousness B is a type of mentality (nāma), not materiality (rūpa). But the question might arise, if consciousness A has already disappeared by the time B observes it, isn't B observing an object from the past? Strictly speaking, yes. But in meditation practice the immediately-preceding consciousness, which is only a split-second in the past, is still considered a present-moment object.

hear the sound, not the bell.

Nāma and rūpa, although fundamental realities, are in continual flux, streaking and vanishing faster than lightning flashes. Under ordinary circumstances, we can't perceive this flux. Yet it is possible, through the practice of insight meditation, to see mind and materiality arising and perishing from moment to moment. Whether we're lying in the sun or running through a storm, nāma and rūpa are ever there. Even as we perceive (apparently) stable boats and trees, the firework-show carries on.

We can't spot neutrons and protons with the naked eye; we see such things as lamps and chairs. And yet, though no one's ever eyed an atom whizzing through the house, who would conclude that his home, with its chairs and lamps, was a neutron-free zone, a maverick exception to the particle world? We are open-minded toward the findings of experts who demonstrate invisible, physical laws. Then there are those who have verified ultimate truth—not by inference, but directly. Couldn't we give them the same benefit of the doubt?

Seurat's painting consists of a single colored surface that can be seen in two ways. Yet the isolated green specks, and the lawn that coalesces when the eye connects them, are not two separate objects. They occupy the same space. But the two views, always there to be seen, are as different in quality as light and dark. Likewise, the conventional and the ultimate exist in the same place—just here, before your eyes, in your own body and mind. Yet their characteristics differ utterly.

Unlike particles and colored specks, however, nāma-rūpa can't be seen by zooming closer in space. One can't prove its existence with instruments. (It's the eye of knowledge, not the physical eye, that perceives it). In a sense, glimpsing ultimate truth is a matter of time rather than space. We can only see it when keeping the mind in the absolute now.

In everyday perception, when an image flips into the line of sight we automatically comprehend it as a named Thing: a tree, a sailboat, an umbrella. But these "things" are only concepts. They aren't what is actually *seen*. "What is seen by ... eye-consciousness," we read in the *Buddhist Dictionary*, "... are colors and differences of light, but not three-dimensional bodily things."[15]

Thinking about color and shape is not seeing. Seeing means contact between the eye and a visual form, which instantly triggers a moment of consciousness. That consciousness—which is extremely brief—experiences the image.[16]

Objects can only be perceived through one of the five sense-organs—the eye, ear, nose, tongue, and body—or the mind itself. In Buddhism these are called sensory "doors". Only one kind of object can enter the eye-door: color. One Buddhist teacher writes, "Color is only the reality which appears through the eyes." We might add, it is the *only* reality which appears through the eyes.

Truly speaking, we have never seen a tree or a boat. To do so would be impossible. What the eye registers is mere tint. Piling words onto momentary blips of visible tint, the mind builds the concepts called "tree," "boat," "sky," and so on. But a mental pastiche is not identical to the experience of pure seeing.

A sailboat on a river, a linden tree, the night sky with its moon—has any one of them ever touched the optic lens? It would be something to see indeed—the moon shooting toward us, tapping against the eye-orb, the two "pool balls" clicking together. In truth the eyes can see only light, manifesting as color. On the other hand, what we call "moon," "boat," "tree," and so on are experienced through the mind-door in a complex process involving memory and conceptual thought.

What is the difference, it might be asked, between viewing Seurat's painting of the park and looking at the "real" thing? In the ultimate sense, none at all. In both cases one sees only color-patches. (Yet no one would deny, in the conventional sense, there is a great difference between looking at a painting and the thing it represents.)

Although it seems that in decades of eyeing the good, the bad and the indifferent we've never beheld exactly the same thing twice, the truth is the reverse: We've been seeing the same thing over and over, and in truth it is neither good nor bad. Is the color red, for instance, inherently good or bad? If it were, we couldn't call it fine in lips and ugly in eyes.

---

15. Nyanatiloka, p. 33.
16. But even within a few seconds of time, many moments of seeing will arise, alternating quickly with thoughts.

CHAPTER 3

A moment ago we separated the tree in the painting from the colored specks that comprised it. Might we now, in our immediate experience, separate the trees, houses, and people we're familiar with from the bare sensory data we're hit with from moment to moment? Impossible, you say? Yet however unlikely it seems, it *is* possible to distinguish pure color from named Things.

Buddhism teaches that visual perception has two phases: 1) seeing, and 2) recognizing. These stages occur very rapidly, one after another. Seeing happens first. No matter what we're looking at, each act of seeing lasts only an instant. In the second phase of perception we recognize and name the object. But the act of naming the image changes it in the mind.

In truth it's only for a moment, at the beginning of each perceptual event, that we see the color as it really is. During that split-second we don't recognize the image but merely apprehend it. Instead of leaves or a branch, we see a color-patch. That unadulterated form is the correct object of mindfulness. It is a real phenomena, not a conceptual one. (Normally we're unable to catch that instant, unable to separate it from the recognition that follows.)

In the next moment we no longer experience pure seeing, because the image is mixed with memory (*saññā*).[17] The mind thinks back to the objects it's known before, as if reasoning, "I've seen something like this—yes, it's called a branch." Yet by the time memory has gone through its inventory and produced a name for the shape, the visual form has already vanished. By the time we dub it *branch*, the moment of pure seeing has fallen away and we perceive an altered image—a mix of remembered color and concepts, but not a present-moment reality.

To recognize a visual object is to "see" by means of memory. One is only aware of the form at the end of the perceptual act, by which time the pure color, the ultimate phenomenon, has been

---

17. *Saññā*, perception, registers an object's distinctive marks. It can also recognize them, functioning as memory.

21

mixed with conceptual knowledge.

The same stages of perception occur whenever we experience a sound, smell, taste or touch. Pure sound-waves are cognized first; in the next moment we recognize the sound. A fragrance is sensed before it is named. The same is true of touches and tastes. In day-to-day life we can't distinguish the stages of perception. Seeing and recognition blur seamlessly together. That's where mindfulness comes in. It is possible, with mindfulness and insight, to stop short at bare seeing before the mind labels the sense-datum—to catch the moment of pure visual reception as it appears and passes away, before we recognize the name. That's what is meant by Just Seeing.[18]

* * *

Our investigation began with a painting. But now let's imagine that we're turning around; turning from the painting in the hall (where the light has grown dim) and moving toward the open window. As we move, new visual shapes spring up.

Now through the window a field can be seen, the grass backlit with the evening sun. A line of poplar trees runs from the field to the house. Something—a squirrel, probably—disappears up the nearest tree, shaking branches as it goes. For a moment our eyes rest there, taking in the gray bark and heart-shaped leaves, noticing how the leaves catch the light when they move. A real tree, this, not a painted one. But what would it be like to Just See it?

All right. Standing before the window we shut our eyes for the count of ten, then quickly open them.

All is changed. The "tree" is gone. As one meditator describes this perceptual shift, "In front of me across the lake, the hazy tree remained a form, and the color as it gradually appeared, was color, and not leaves and branches."[19] Only lines and patches of tint

---

18. According to Bhikkhu Anālayo, the Bāhiya instruction, "directs bare awareness to whatever is seen, heard, sensed, or cognized ... This corresponds to an interception of the first stages in the sequence of the perceptual process, through mindful attention." *Satipaṭṭhāna*, p. 230. Despite our use of the word "catch," it is the duty of mindfulness, not the ego, to stop at the bare sense-datum.
19. Shattock, *Experiment in Mindfulness*, p. 69.

appear, as if the color had peeled away from its background. The shapes don't represent anything—the color is color *merely* Even the hues are not recognized as "gray" or "green." A guy-wire to content has been cut and there is only, "pure sensation unencumbered by meaning."

Perhaps this makes Just Seeing sound easy, as if one could do it at will; but here is where the example is misleading. In truth, no one can decide, "now I'm going to Just See". The event can't be forced but only occurs spontaneously, when the right conditions of mind are present. You (meaning, your desire and ego) can't Just See, but mindfulness (*sati*) and wisdom (*paññā*) can. This means that you—what you think of as your self—can't will *sati* and *paññā* to arise on demand, just as you couldn't become a champion swimmer merely by wishing it. To realize that aim you'd have to undergo training. But that isn't to say we are helpless. Just Seeing does not depend on chance. The mind can be trained as well as the body. Mindfulness and wisdom can be cultivated through the Eightfold Path.

It is not possible, during a moment of Just Seeing, to recognize conventional Things like trees, grasslands, or even our own hands. "If we could focus precisely on the present moment," one vipassanā teacher writes, "... the eye would not be able to identify objects coming into the area of perception."[20] At the moment of pure visual reception, the mind has yet to paste a concept on the image. If mindfulness is fast enough to catch the initial phase of perception, the meditator knows only hue. The same holds true for the other sense-impressions. One is only aware of the continuous arising and ceasing of pure phenomena, which leaves no opening for concepts to form.

The English monk Kapilavaddho Bhikkhu described his foray into Just Seeing: "The experience," he wrote, "came about quite naturally ... At the time I was casually looking at my left hand, when suddenly ... The hand had lost all sense of solidity ... Here, all that was presented to the eye was color." This echoes Mahāsi

---

20. Achan Sobin Namto, *Wayfaring*, p. 15. If we focus on the present moment, he adds, "Sound ... would not be concretized as speech or music, etc. In fact, it is possible to focus on the split-second between hearing sound and recognizing it." Ibid.

Sayādaw's statement, when infused with strong mindfulness, "The observing mind promptly notes every phenomenon as it occurs, leaving no room for the illusion of hand, leg, and so forth."[21]

Normally we think, "*I* am seeing." But although seeing and hearing occur every minute, in truth there is no self who carries out these actions. When Just Seeing, the I-feeling is absent. Although there is awareness of each experience, there's no sense it is happening to "me". From this we discover that a self is not essential to perception.

It isn't a self who sees, but consciousness. Contrary to popular opinion, consciousness doesn't equal an *I*. It is, in truth, momentary and impersonal. According to the Buddhist teachings, the flow of consciousness is not an unbroken stream but a series of separate moments that arise and vanish, one after another, with incredible speed. No self or soul carries over from one perceptual act to the next. The mind that sees something quickly dies, and a different consciousness hears a sound. The mind is born over and over every moment. It dies over and over, too.

We read in the *Buddhist Dictionary*:

> Strictly speaking ... death is the continually repeated dissolution and vanishing of each momentary physical-mental combination (nāma-rūpa), and thus it takes place every moment ... "For it is said: 'The being of the past moment of consciousness has lived, but does not live now, nor will it live in future. The being of the future moment has not yet lived, nor does it live now, but it will live in the future. The being of the present moment has not lived, it does live just now, but it will not live in the future.'" (Nyanatiloka, p. 114–5)

When one instant of seeing is over, mind and color vanish; then another nāma-rūpa appears, immediately. That is the nature of life. Color, sound, and other phenomena, along with the units of consciousness that know them, keep forming and passing away in an ongoing chain. The meditator simply notes the next blip of sound, color or movement that arises. He doesn't use force to counteract the tendency to conceptualize. The impulse to build

21. Randall, *Siamese Monk*, pp. 120–1; Mahāsi Sayādaw, *Dependent Origination*, p. 8 (hereafter cited in text).

concepts is naturally prevented when the student brings awareness back to the present moment, over and over again. When we stop short at bare perception before any concepts arise to complicate it, the truth of nonself becomes clearer and clearer, since it is the reality, always there to be known.

When a meditator Just Sees or Hears, no unwholesome mind-states arise, since no misperception occurs. Because consciousness stays with the present moment of experience, delusion has no chance to form. In the absence of delusion, desire and hatred cannot appear. Even if it's only for a single moment, the benefit of Just Seeing (or Just Knowing any object) can surpass the highest, mundane boon.[22] If wisdom is strong enough, so it is said, the result of a few successive moments is even greater, for right there one can enter the stream to Nibbāna.

Let's look at another example. Suppose, from a single tube of red pigment, an artist paints two pictures; one depicts a vase of poppies, the other, a dress stained with blood. We might admire the poppies but dislike the bloody dress (or the other way around). Yet both paintings were created from the same pigment. The image of the poppies didn't spring from a tube labeled "Red Lovely," that of the dress from one stamped "Red Ugly." Why prefer one picture to the other? Beauty and its opposite don't reside in material form. They are meanings twisted up after the fact, by the mind.

During a moment of Just Seeing, we wouldn't think the *word* "red," "scarlet" or "flower" when viewing the poppies, or the word "blood" when looking at the other picture. There would be no impulse to name the shapes. Nor would there be any interest in the aspect of perception that obsesses us in daily life: the details of the shape, the mundane meaning of the image. Neither the positive connotations of poppies nor the negative associations of blood could affect us while eyeing the forms (such judgments can't arise when the mind stays in the immediate present).

Just Seeing a color-patch generates no thoughts *about* it—indeed, generates no thoughts at all. After knowing the image for an instant, the mind lets go. It doesn't cling to the object even for a second.

---

22. If, during this experience, a person discerns impermanence, suffering or nonself clearly, he usually cannot be reborn in the lower realms in his next life. See p. 82.

The longer we look at an image with ordinary perception, the more it seems to differ from other objects. Yet it's because of unwise attention to the details of forms—all sensory forms, not just sights—that liking, disliking and clinging arise. Most beings, of course, have a mouth and eyes. But when we see a person, the mind doesn't always stop there. It describes and compares in fine detail, dwelling on the most insignificant differences. "I like the way her mouth turns up at the corners." "His eyes are too small." Never mind that others find the mouth ugly or the eyes appealing. The mind issues its verdicts; the gavel falls—to the defilements (the mental impurities desire, hatred and delusion).

But when Just Seeing, mundane differences fall away. The mind is unaware of them as it bends instead toward the ultimate aspects of the image. Insight knows that every tinted shape is essentially the same.

We read in the suttas: "And how, friend, does one guard the doors of the sense faculties? Here, having seen a form with the eye, a bhikkhu does not grasp its signs and features" (SN 35:120).[23] Instead of relishing the mundane features of an image (the individual details of shape and color) the meditator ignores them, focusing instead on what is routinely passed over: the knowing itself, the *act* of cognizing the tint. The focus is on the seeing, not merely on the object seen. The student is aware of the knower as well as the known, observing the mind as-it-apprehends-the-color.

Stripped of its conventional meaning, a color-patch is not an abstraction. On the contrary, the concepts we impose after seeing it are the abstractions, having no reality in the absolute sense. Erase the descriptions and we're left with ultimate truth: a momentary, impersonal image (rūpa) that doesn't pertain to any named thing beyond itself; and the mind (nāma), which is there to know the sensation.

"I began to realize after *seeing* in this new manner," Kapilavaddho Bhikkhu writes, "that the 'object' of sight was purely a matter of color. Of itself it was neither pleasant nor unpleasant, desirable nor undesirable, harmful nor harmless ... The only real I could find was in the data presented in the act of sight before the

---

23. On "signs and features," see Bhikkhu Bodhi, *Connected Discourses*, p. 1127; and Mahāsi Sayādaw, *Progress of Insight*, p. 22.

mind had added its terms and concepts."[24]

Just Seeing means to catch the instant when color contacts the retina, before memory tags it as white or green, or a sail or a leaf. The mind leaves the experience as is without identifying, interpreting or imposing any bias. This accords with the Buddha's words, "On seeing, let seeing be" (SN 35:95).

When we let things be, craving can't pull us about. The mind, ceasing to get emotionally involved in the forms seen and heard, remains at ease. No agitation arises from the contact of eye and image, or ear and sound. That doesn't mean suppressing sensation through deep concentration (*jhāna*). We are still aware of sense-impressions, but the mind stops short before liking and disliking can stir up suffering.[25]

In a broader sense, "stopping short" refers to the repetitive effort to return to the present moment. A meditator, when he notices the mind falling into the past or dreaming about the future, gently tugs on the leash to bring it back to *now.* Whenever consciousness wanders out to think about something, he sweeps it back to the present moment where a new sight, sound or movement is already erupting. The vigilance maintained is continuous yet relaxed. Even in the case of emotions or thoughts, he doesn't force them away, but merely observes.

Here a word should be said about concepts. When an image is experienced in the conventional way, as a relatively lasting, named Thing, we are perceiving a concept. A concept cannot literally be seen with the eyes, since it isn't a visual form.

There is nothing wrong with experiencing concepts. This point is often misunderstood. In daily life, conceptual thinking is not only useful but essential. Without it we couldn't even safely cross the street. The problem comes when we don't *know* we're beholding a concept when perceiving a boat, leaf, teapot and so on. Most of us invariably take the concepts for absolute entities.

Mistaking the shadows of real things for the things themselves leads to erroneous views about mind and matter. That's because

---

24. Randall, *Siamese Monk*, pp. 121–2.

25. In regard to stopping at the bare sense-datum, see Bhikkhu Bodhi, *Connected Discourses*, p. 1127; and Mahāsi Sayādaw, *Discourse on Mālukyaputta*, p. 22. (Hereafter cited in text as "*Mālukyaputta*.")

concepts tend to conceal the ultimate characteristics—impermanence, unsatisfactoriness and nonselfness—common to all phenomena.

But to cease conceptualizing altogether isn't the answer. What is needed, if we're to know the phenomenal world with any accuracy, is to recognize concepts as such and distinguish them from the pure images, sounds and other sensory data that flash up for a moment, like, "raindrops soon dried by the wind."

Up to now we have talked mostly of seeing, but in practice a meditator should note every phenomenon that brushes against awareness, not only sights. Everything we've said so far about color applies to all the objects of direct experience. During vipassanā practice we Just Hear sound, Just Smell fragrance, Just Taste flavor, and Just Touch tactile forms with bare attention. All sense-perceptions are phenomenal darts of equal value—only flashes of sensation for the mind to know and let go of.

But the objects we focus on the most during formal meditation are in fact touches, since they are the easiest to watch. Tactile impressions are not limited to sensations of pressure, heat or cold from outside objects contacting the skin. Bodily motion—the movement of the hand or leg, for instance—is also experienced through the tactile sense, and constitutes the main meditation object in vipassanā practice.

But what if, despite understanding the theory, we still have doubts about Just Seeing, Hearing, Touching, and so forth? Perhaps it seems impossible to do. Mahāsi Sayādaw writes, "Some people who have never meditated may have some doubt, which is hardly surprising for only seeing is believing. Their skepticism is due to their lack of experience."[26] Even some people who later become meditation teachers are dubious at first. The bhikkhu Achan Sobin Namto believed Just Seeing impossible until he experienced it firsthand.[27] Afterwards he spent more than fifty years teaching the "Bāhiya" technique to others.

Indeed, Mahāsi Sayādaw himself had doubts. "I was skeptical at one time, too," he says. "I did not then like the [meditation] method ... However ... I decided to give it a trial. At first I made

---

26. *Discourse on the Ariyavatta Sutta*, p. 7.
27. Personal communication with the author.

little progress because I had lingering doubts ... It was only later, when I had followed the [Four Foundations of Mindfulness] method seriously, that its significance dawned on me. I realized then that it is the best method of meditation since it calls for attentiveness to everything that can be known, leaving no room for absent-mindedness."[28]

The only way to know if Just Seeing is really possible (to say nothing of Nibbāna) is to practice meditation ourselves. We should not believe it is beyond our capabilities to Just See. It is within reach of everyone, male or female, young or old, who earnestly wants to know the truth. No special aptitude is needed, only the right training. But what is true or false can't be reasoned out beforehand, because ultimate reality concerns direct vision, not conceptual knowledge. Many features of reality seem implausible until we taste the dhamma[29] directly; then all the doubts and questions disappear.

* * *

Someone might wonder, if Just Seeing means to perceive unnamed color patches, isn't it a kind of regression to infancy, a passive un-knowing? And if that's the case, what makes it more than a curious experiment? How does it differ from the perceptions of babes in the crib?

Merely seeing pure visual form, or hearing sound without recognizing the words, is not the objective of meditation. The objective of insight meditation is liberation from suffering. To achieve that aim, one must directly experience the impermanence of sights, sounds and other sense-impressions.

In order to realize impermanence *directly* (rather than merely thinking about it) it is necessary to intercept the flow of consciousness with mindfulness and insight. So doing suspends, temporarily, the unwholesome mental factors that distort perception in the first place. That window of time free of delusion

---

28. *Discourse on the Ariyavatta Sutta*, p. 7. The "Four Foundations of Mindfulness" (*Satipaṭṭhāna*) refer to the objects for developing sati, i.e.: 1) the body, 2) feelings, 3) consciousness, and 4) mind-objects.
29. "Dhamma" has many meanings, one of which is the true nature of realities, both conditioned (nāma-rūpa) and unconditioned (Nibbāna).

and craving allows us to see phenomena in line with ultimate truth. (Delusion is eliminated permanently when one attains full enlightenment.) It is not unknowing, but using mindfulness and insight to glimpse the ultimate features of reality, features that had not been apparent before.

As everyone knows, when an infant perceives a color-patch, he does not regard it in terms of a "crib," a "teddy bear," or some other conventional concept. And yet we've all seen babies reach out to grasp objects that please them. The infant is attracted to the visual form and wants to obtain it. Just as with adults, desire arises because the child does not know that the swatch of tint is momentary, arising merely to pass away the same instant, and that it cannot truly be owned.

If it is to count as Just Seeing, visual forms must be known in light of their impermanent, impersonal and ownerless nature. With such right understanding our infatuation with sights will necessarily diminish, not increase.[30]

The Malaysian teacher Ven. Sujīva writes, "Merely directing the mind towards realities is usually not sufficient. One has to direct one's attentions towards the sign of impermanence that is inherent in the realities."[31] That does not mean imposing a preconceived agenda on seeing and hearing (in the way concepts are superimposed on phenomena), but priming the mind with right view so that mindfulness and wisdom can discern the attributes already present in those objects.

It might be asked, what is meant by the word "impermanence" (*anicca*) in Buddhism? Answer: *Momentaneity.* Suppose you are half-way through watching a television program. How long would you say you'd been looking at the screen? Half an hour? An hour? Ultimately speaking, the act of seeing does not last the hours or

---

30. Mahāsi Sayādaw remarks, "In fact, merely perceiving forms and shapes does not amount to self-clinging. Neither does no longer perceiving shapes and forms mean that knowledge of not-self is established." *Great Discourse on Not Self*, p. 12. (Hereafter cited in text as "*Great Discourse*.") An enlightened person can know conventional shapes without the false idea they are part of his self. Conversely, merely perceiving color-patches as infants do without seeing their impermanence will not erase the belief in self.

31. *Wisdom Treasury,* p. 8. (Hereafter cited in text.)

minutes we think it does. Each instance of visual perception bursts like a bubble even as it appears, lasting no longer than a fraction of a second. It seems we can look at something for minutes at a stretch only because many perceptual acts arise in quick succession.

In saying that each instance of perception vanishes on the spot, we aren't speaking metaphorically. When insight is strong the mind's eye can actually *see* impermanence, as clearly as seeing a soap bubble break. One can assume the average newborn sees no such burst when eyeing his bear.

A meditator who clearly sees phenomena vanishing in the immediate present has reached the level of insight called "knowledge of dissolution." This experience is literally like watching, "the quick and continuous bursting of bubbles produced in a heavy shower by thick rain drops falling on a water surface."[32]

Knowledge of dissolution is key, because only by seeing the immediate, moment-to-moment disappearance of sights and sounds can we become disenchanted with them. That disenchantment is a necessary precursor to realizing Nibbāna. (This is one feature that differentiates the meditator's experience from the infant's.)

Most of us want to have our cake and eat it, too. Although we are glad to learn that painful sensations are impermanent, we don't want the pleasant ones to change. Deep down we still believe pleasure can be made, if not permanent, at least relatively lasting. No one could reasonably expect good sensations to endure forever, but we'd be satisfied (so we tell ourselves) if they lasted *long enough*—whether that means a few years, days or hours. So we continue to latch on to pleasant sights and sounds, living under the illusion they are worth going after. But if we ever hope to end craving and reach a happiness superior to temporary pleasure, something must—pardon the pun—burst our bubble. That "something" is the direct knowledge of the momentary nature of mind and matter.

It is one thing to remind ourselves that beloved objects and people last no more than a few years, quite another to watch a pleasant formation die out in less than a tick of the clock. When

---

32. Mahāsi Sayādaw, *Progress of Insight*, p. 23. Dissolution-knowledge is the 5th of the 16 levels of insight. To be genuine it must be seen directly, not just imagined or thought about.

people realize, "things do not endure even for a second and are constantly dissolving," writes Mahāsi Sayādaw, "they can no longer see any ... goodness in them" (*Great Discourse*, p. 99). Only then is it possible to let go of craving and know a higher kind of happiness.

Mahāsi Sayādaw emphasizes the link between the experience of dissolution when Just Seeing and the growing knowledge of the three characteristics (impermanence, suffering, and nonselfness). "Having gained experience of dissolution," he says, "the meditator will benefit from direct knowledge of impermanence. This will lead to the revelation that what is not permanent is unsatisfactory and insubstantial, as one has virtually no control over mind and matter" (*Mālukyaputta*, p. 18).[33] Not until this level of insight can these characteristics be known clearly enough to make a real dent in our mistaken views. "According to the *Visuddhimagga* [*The Path of Purification*], it is only this knowledge of dissolution that enables the meditator to overcome thoroughly the illusions of permanence, pleasantness, and ego-entity."[34]

In regard to the experience of dissolution, we should point out that conventional objects such as chairs and trees do not pop like balloons as we watch them. On the contrary, it is the hallmark of conventional forms to appear enduring and stable. Conversely, when seeing dissolution we do not at the same time perceive the conventional signs. What we see disappearing is mere sensation, nāma-rūpa.

Looking again at Seurat's painting, we find it is possible to shift the eye rather quickly between the two views. As the specks come into focus the trees vanish. When our gaze pans back out, the scattered dots jump to attention, forming the familiar shapes of trees and boats. The eye can alternate back and forth quite rapidly.

Although we cannot experience ultimate truth and conventional reality at the same moment, it is possible to experience them one after another in consecutive moments. When looking at an object we may, for that instant, see visible form arising

---

33. See also Mahāsi Sayādaw, *Discourse on the Sallekha Sutta*, p. 152. Hereafter given as *"Sallekha Sutta."*
34. Mahāsi Sayādaw, *Sallekha Sutta*, p. 266; see also *Great Discourse*, p. 98, and Tullius, *Vipassanā Bhāvanā*, p. 91.

and passing away. In the next moment the mind may gear down to conventional consciousness and recognize the image as a sail or a twig, at the same time grasping the name of the thing. It is possible for these experiences to arise sequentially within the space of a few seconds. "So one comes to know by direct experience the truth of the wise saying: When a name or designation arises, a reality lies hidden; when a reality reveals itself, a name or designation disappears."[35]

Until the final exit from saṃsāra (the round of rebirth), which might be several lifetimes away, consciousness may continue to shift between the ultimate and the conventional, sometimes from one moment to the next. (However, what we perceive at any given moment does not always correspond to our intention. What is experienced depends on conditions.) Mahāsi Sayādaw offers a lovely simile for the mind's return to ultimate reality: "Those who have gained insight knowledge, but have stopped noting the three characteristics for some time, can regain their insight soon after they resume their practice. This is like returning to one's home." Although desire and ill-will may arise when mindfulness is weak, once these students regain mindfulness, "they will retrieve their insight into the truth. It is like leaving the comfort and security of one's home, to visit several places during the day for some reason and returning for the night."[36]

The mind can stay with ordinary reality when necessary, working and conversing, and at other times glimpse nāma-rūpa, without clinging to either view. Even Nibbāna should not be clung to. As the Thai teacher Achan Kor wrote, "The Buddha's teaching ... 'All phenomena are not-self,' tells us not to latch on to any of the phenomena of nature, whether conditioned or conditionless."[37]

35. Mahāsi Sayādaw, *Practical Insight*, p. 27. Hereafter cited in text.
36. *Discourse on Hemavata Sutta*, pp. 57–8.
37. Kor Khao Suan Luang, *Looking Inward*, p. 51.

CHAPTER 4

Paintings, windows, mirrors—all have frames. Although by the world's standards they're different, the patches of tint caught between wood or gilt borders, or framed in the mirror above the bathroom sink, are perfectly equal in ultimate terms, all being rūpa. Does the color black have an ego, a self? The image seen in the mirror, the image called "the pupil of my eye," is only a dot of black tint. Does that jot of black color differ from another? There's no tag attached reading "property of self." Blackness possesses the same properties wherever it appears. The dot in the mirror is no more nor less black, and has no more to do with an I, than a black speck in Seurat's print.

White and yellow can't be angry. But suppose the sight of an angry store clerk sparks annoyance or hurt. Why, one wonders, is he rude to *me*? Conventionally speaking, we're looking at a scowling clerk. But what are we really seeing? Can we swing our gaze around and view the scene in ultimate terms?

From this perspective we find, rather than a person, we're seeing an arrangement of hue—white, brown, yellow or other tints—phenomena that can't become irate. All that's really happened is that a particular configuration of color, a visual sign called a "face," has twisted into a slightly different shape. We see a flat appearance in which some bands of tint have bent downwards by a few degrees, while others have shifted a few points to the left or right—innocuous occurrences, to be sure. Is the slight alteration of a few color-patches ample cause for getting upset? Do such trivia warrant the toppling of an already-shaky peace of mind?

"But," you protest, "I'm seeing a *person*, not an abstract artwork." Precisely. It's because we perceive a person instead of color we feel upset. When seeing things only from the conventional side, the mind often gets distressed. But when seeing reality in ultimate terms, we can't get angry. The mind doesn't suffer.

Ultimately speaking, the image of the clerk isn't the extension of a person in space, the anterior surface behind which a conniving self is concealed. There's no permanent being behind the appearance. No soul can claim the moving shape we dub a "face."[38]

The eye cannot see a self, because a self is not a visible object, nor is consciousness. Even if it were, each stream of consciousness is also impersonal, comprised of momentary conditions erupting and dying from second to second. But in failing to know reality from the ultimate standpoint we can't help getting involved, can't resist interpreting a swoosh of tint as a snub and then feeling annoyed.

And yet, if considered thoughtfully, we might admit that the visual sign called "an angry face" doesn't actually hurt the eyes as staring at the sun does. Perhaps the sound called "the clerk's voice" gets louder, but it doesn't physically hurt the ear as sitting beside a blaring speaker would. The injured feeling arises not from the rūpa seen or heard, but from our attachment to its conventional meaning.

This is most easily understood, perhaps, with hearing. In order to function in the world, of course, we must know the meaning of the sounds we hear. But there are exceptions, and at such times we can use skillful means. When an angry person abuses us it isn't necessary to know the meaning of each word. If we mindfully note the act of hearing, rather than attending to the meaning of the sound, suffering can't arise when someone utters harsh words. Nor will we react with anger. The mind stays calm and the mouth quiet. "In my native village," Mahāsi Sayādaw writes:

> there is a meditator who is very mindful ... While he was a layman he noted, "hearing, hearing," whenever he heard his father-in-law rebuking him ... To him [the layman] the voice of the speaker as well as his words disappeared instantly and he did not know anything about what the old man was saying. He was not angry nor did he have any desire to retort. However, if not for his mindfulness, he would have retorted angrily and uttered harsh words.[39]

Achan Sobin remarks that once, during a meditation retreat, he

---

38. Sujin Boriharnwanaket says, in the ultimate sense, "When we see somebody, we should know that this is in reality the same as seeing a picture, thus, we know in both cases a concept." *Realities and Concepts*.
39. Mahāsi Sayādaw, *Sallekha Sutta*, pp. 113–4.

failed to recognize the sound of his own name being called. "Everyone thought I had gone crazy", he said. But he explains that it was due to the strength of mindfulness, which kept stopping at the bare sense-datum, that the mind failed to recognize the meaning of the sound. (Later, of course, he again recognized his name.)[40]

If we focus on the *act* of hearing, sound cannot hurt us. But normally the mind clings to the conventional view. Out of sound and color, mere impersonal elements, it fashions a drama entangled in the rigging of self. And so we suffer.

How often have we seen an actor display the signs of anger? But since we don't interpret *them* as genuine or pertaining to our self, the exhibition doesn't faze us. We might even laugh.

The audience isn't hurt by an actor's rage. Can we likewise become spectators to the daily display of sights and sounds? If the mind could separate ultimate reality from the conventional we could let the twisting plots run past without getting entangled. Events small and large would glide by without causing distress.

But someone might still object that in the example of the clerk we're speaking of a person, not a Picasso. Isn't it solipsistic and lacking in compassion to regard people as mere constellations of phenomena? In a word, no. To understand, in the *ultimate* sense, beings are only streams of nāma-rūpa, void of self, does not mean we will treat them as inanimate paintings. On the contrary—when the knots of attachment are loosened, compassion can flow freely. One then has more consideration for other beings, not less. The Buddha declared that suffering exists, even though there's no self to which the suffering pertains (it's the suffering of conditions, not a self); and the more deeply we understand ultimate reality, the more we'll shrink from causing distress, whether to bird, beast or man.

A genuine insight into ultimate truth does not lead to harmful behavior. There is no reason to fear, when seeing only color, one would lose all qualms about doing something wrong. Delusion, remember, cannot arise when Just Seeing. Of all the unwholesome mental factors that taint the mind, delusion is the subtlest. If delusion cannot arise, neither can greed or anger, much coarser

---

40. Interview with the author. See http://www.vipassanadhura.com/edmontonthree.htm for a fuller account.

mental factors. It is impossible to have a harmful intention when Just Seeing, because the mind at that moment is pure, entirely free of unwholesome or destructive emotions, in a state of total equanimity. As Mahāsi Sayādaw writes, "No defilements [mental impurities] can arise on realizing the true nature of impermanent phenomena" (*Mālukyaputta*, p. 24).

It is possible to conquer animosity permanently by practicing mindfulness. "When we see a person whom we do not want to see, or when we hear a sound that we do not wish to hear," Mahāsi Sayādaw explains, "... we have ill-will, 'Damn that fellow! A plague on him!' However, with mindfulness at every moment of seeing, hearing, etc., you will find that every thought and feeling passes away instantly—then it is impossible for ill-will to arise."[41]

Seeing color instead of a clerk is not a detached fantasy to talk ourselves into, a bubble by which to insulate from hurts. It isn't a case of intellectualizing. On the contrary, everyday perception is the intellectualization. Bare color and other sense-impressions are experience unadulterated: the raw, primal reality. Nāma-rūpa must be seen directly, not merely imagined or believed in. When ultimate truth is seen clearly we'll know we have woken up to the realest reality.

However, we are not suggesting a person roam forever through a desert of empty tint, blundering into people and objects he doesn't recognize. The aim is not to dispense with conventional perception altogether. The obligatory mode of everyday life, it allows us to communicate with others, earn a living, and otherwise negotiate the avenues of the world. Even the Buddhist teachings must be learned through conventional labels. ("It is with concepts that we learn to turn to realities," Ven. Sujīva remarks.) What is sobering to remember, however, is that most of us view mind and matter through a shell of ignorance that is never, even for a moment, pierced. For that reason we do not know the deeper truth about our world.

When the film *The Arrival of the Train* was screened in 1895, some audience-members rushed to the back of the room, presumably afraid a real train was coming toward them. Although they correctly identified the shape of the image onscreen, it was believed to be

---

41. *Sallekha Sutta*, p. 125.

more than a picture—substantial, even dangerous. Likewise, those who lack mindfulness and insight, misled by perception's conjuring-trick, believe mind and matter to be relatively lasting, desirable, and amenable to ownership. Mahāsi Sayādaw remarks:

> Just as a mirage gives the illusion of a body of water or of houses where no such things exist, so also *saññā* (perception) deceives people into thinking that whatever is seen, heard, touched or known is [for example] a human being, a man or a woman. With their illusory perceptions ... people become involved in multiple activities concerning them, just like the deer of the wild forests who go after a distant mirage, taking it to be a mass of water. (*Great Discourse*, p. 72)

But those who develop insight to the point of seeing through the conventions can still watch the movie, still function in the everyday world, without falling into the wrong view that phenomena are permanent, personal, and worthy of being wanted. Those individuals can experience concepts without being misled by them. That reduces their suffering substantially. Even one instant of perception charged with wisdom is immensely beneficial. "When one can penetrate to the truth of impermanence, suffering and not-self, even if just for a moment," says Tan Achan Kor, "one sees that this is truly the perfect way to extinguish all suffering ... Just a momentary insight gives value to one's life, otherwise one remains in the continual darkness of ignorance and ceaseless imaginings."[42]

Daily life requires that we conceptualize about the sights and sounds around us. Does that mean we cannot be mindful during everyday activities? No, it does not. Mindfulness is a conditioned mental factor which fluctuates, having degrees from weak to strong. Mahāsi Sayādaw explains:

> At first, however, the meditator will find it difficult to apprehend the [ultimate] reality because mindfulness, concentration, and wisdom are not yet strong enough. When these qualities become firmly established, the meditator will be able to realize the true nature of things. (*Mālukyaputta*, p. 15)

---

42. Kor Khao Suan Luang, *Directing to Self-Penetration*, p. 17.

Although mindfulness (*sati*) is not developed in the beginner, it is nevertheless implied he possesses it. Since a beginner still perceives conventional objects when meditating, but admittedly has mindfulness, one concludes that a person can still be mindful when observing concepts.

But we have to distinguish between two types of *sati*: 1) the ordinary, general type that knows a conventional object (some call this "awareness"); and 2) the strong mindfulness that knows an ultimate object (nāma or rūpa) in the immediate present, with bare attention.[43] The difference is a matter of degree and, in the second, the presence of supporting factors such as concentration and wisdom.

In daily life we usually have ordinary mindfulness. But Just Seeing, Hearing and Knowing require the second type. This stronger *sati* occurs less frequently—only, at first, in isolated moments of split-second duration. It can't be induced by deciding to pay attention, as you might pay attention to the movement of your arm. Those moments of keen mindfulness can't be willed or anticipated. (One writer calls them, "very elusive, like trying to catch a fish in a pond with the hands.")

But if strong *sati* depends on a host of elusive conditions that can't be manipulated, why make the effort to be mindful? Again, although conditions cannot be made to stretch or shrink on demand, they aren't random. If we know what the causes for strong mindfulness are, we can make the effort to generate them.

A meditator isn't foolish. He wouldn't run into oncoming traffic or plunge his hand in a fire because, "it's just color." Most of the time during daily activities he still perceives conventional realities (although he is more mindful of his thoughts, motivations and

---

43. We might call the second "vipassanā-mindfulness." Several contemporary vipassanā teachers mention two kinds of sati. A disciple of the late Achan Naeb writes, "There are two satis: ... 1) Normal, or mundane, sati would be to do any ... (wholesome action) with awareness—such as giving food to monks, etc. 2) Sati in satipaṭṭhāna (vipassanā) practice is sati in which the object is seen as rūpa or nāma, in the present moment." Tullius, *Vipassanā Bhavana*, p. 38. Achan Sobin calls the first type "awareness," the second, "mindfulness." See also Ayya Khema, *When the Iron Eagle Flies*, p. 182. On right and wrong mindfulness, see Mahāsi Sayādaw, *Sallekha Sutta*, p. 170-2.

sense-impressions than most folks are). At such times he is aware of concepts. Yet *in between* the moments of knowing concepts, a flash of keen mindfulness can arise that knows rūpa or nāma. The more we cultivate mindfulness and wisdom, the more those spontaneous moments will occur, like short bursts between stretches of everyday perception.

But is the second type of *sati* necessary? What happens if we only note conventional realities? For example: "Now I'm touching the desk ... hearing the cathedral bells ... eating a pear ... washing a plate"? Here the mind isn't daydreaming or ruminating. It knows when you are eating a pear as opposed to washing a plate. In this manner you may develop some insight—but not enough to make nonselfness truly *clear*. This level of knowledge does not cut deeply enough to make you tire of pleasant sights, sounds and tastes. As Tan Achan Kor wrote:

> If you keep watch on bare arising and disbanding you're sure to arrive at insight. But if you keep watch with labels—'That's the sound of a cow,' 'That's the bark of a dog,'—you won't be watching the bare sensation of sound, the bare sensation of arising and disbanding. As soon as there's labeling, thought-formations come along with it ... and then there will be attachments, feelings of pleasure and displeasure, and you won't know the truth.[44]

That's not to say we should disregard ordinary mindfulness. Along with clear comprehension (right or suitable knowledge),[45] it can support the arising of stronger *sati*. Whether we are raking leaves, rinsing the dishes or walking to work, we should know our movements and changing states of mind. But why stop there? The fact is, if the aim is to reach Nibbāna, mindfulness of events in the conventional sense is necessary but not sufficient.

---

44. Kor Khao Suan Luang, *Looking Inward*, pp. 41–2 (hereafter cited in text). "Arising and disbanding" refers to the moment-to-moment appearing and vanishing of sights, sounds, etc.

45. An example of clear comprehension in daily life would be to consider whether an action or remark were beneficial before executing it. In formal vipassanā practice, clear comprehension is equivalent to insight-knowledge. It exists on a continuum with wisdom (*paññā*), although the latter is a much intensified form.

What if you resolved to study Seurat's painting, but could only view it from ten yards away—would it matter how many years you stood gazing? How would you *ever* learn that the boats and trees, solid things-in-themselves from where you stood, weren't in the least solid—were, in fact, riddled with gaps? There are things that just can't be seen without moving closer.

Distance matters in time as well as space. Those who have not experienced the pure present are liable to perceive the world as a collection of enduring Beings and Things. Many temporal dots are run together, blurring their momentaneity. By the time we register a handful of them, the sleight-of-hand called *self*, and various tricks of good and bad, have already occurred. That's why, "When you turn to look inward, you shouldn't use concepts and labels to do your looking for you. If you use concepts and labels to do your looking, there will be nothing but concepts arising, changing and disbanding" (ibid., p. 45).

Right understanding is essential if we want to experience ultimate reality, because it will help promote the arising of stronger mindfulness and insight. What is right understanding in the context of insight meditation? In part it is to recognize, if only intellectually at first, the difference between concepts and ultimate realities, and to know that the aim in vipassanā is to observe the latter, with bare attention. Beyond that it means knowing that each sensation, each flare of movement, color, or sound is an impersonal phenomenon—not owned by you (or anyone).

In the beginning, the objects noted during meditation will be conventional. We can't expect to see ultimate realities from day one. But knowing that the goal is to observe bare phenomena without verbalization will keep us on the right path. So even if we can't yet separate pure color and sound from the veneer of concepts in practice, our effort should be aimed in that direction. The mind won't cling to labels any longer than necessary when right understanding supports effort. Otherwise the misconception of a self who sees, touches and hears will be hard to uproot.

"It is no easy matter," Mahāsi Sayādaw writes, "to stop short at just seeing. A beginner will not be able to catch the thought moments that make up the process of seeing" (*Mālukyaputta*, p. 14). That's why training is required. Although mindfulness is not something to relegate to a special hour and then abandon, neither should we swing to the other extreme and underestimate the value of time given solely to its cultivation. Although general mindfulness and clear comprehension are helpful in daily life, during the hour devoted exclusively to vipassanā practice we will be free to drop the conventional labels and Just Know sensations with bare attention—without being concerned we might let the rice boil over, cut a finger, or set the house on fire. It's a chance for the mind to really let go, to lay down the burdens of judgment and comparison it carries all day. "If you can keep watch in this way," says Tan Achan Kor, "you're with the pure present—and there won't be any issues ... you're keeping watch on inconstancy, on change, as it actually occurs" (*Looking Inward*, p. 41).

In order to realize even the first level of awakening, a meditator must pass each rung on the ladder of insight. There are sixteen rungs in all.[46] Conventional forms still appear at the earlier levels, but as the mind climbs higher they fall away. (But not permanently. We can still access the names and concepts when needed.) The line of demarcation, if you will, is the stage mentioned earlier, "knowledge of dissolution." As Mahāsi Sayādaw explains:

> Mindfulness does not lead to insight at once, but while contemplating mind and matter, one develops strong concentration and vigilant mindfulness, leaving little room for stray thoughts ... Even so, conventional notions linger before the attainment of knowledge of dissolution [insight No. 5]. So it is said in the *Visuddhimagga* that at the earlier stage of insight [No. 4], the meditator sees, ' ... the lights and flowers on the pagoda platform, or fishes and turtles in the sea.' Later, however, both the ... objects of contemplation and the contemplating mind are found to pass away repeatedly. Conventional ideas such as name or form do not arise any longer. As the *Visuddhimagga* says, 'attention is fixed on cessation, disappearance, and dissolution.'[47] (*Dependent Origination*, pp. 79–80)

This passage shows the importance of the second type of mindfulness for attaining the higher stages of insight. In order to progress beyond the fourth level of insight-knowledge,

---

46. Although 16 levels are usually described, in *Progress of Insight* Mahāsi Sayādaw divides level 12 into two stages, for a total of 17.
47. Conventional ideas arise again when the student stops meditating.

mindfulness must observe ultimate realities for a period of time. How long that time must be varies according to the innate wisdom of each meditator. For Bāhiya, mere seconds was enough.

In addition to the strength of mindfulness itself, we should take into account supporting factors such as concentration. "The true nature of the psychophysical process", Mahāsi Sayādaw remarks, "can be realized only by a mindful person. However, this insight does not occur initially when concentration is undeveloped" (ibid., p. 8).

Just Seeing or Hearing occurs when mindfulness is strong and its supporting factors harmonized. That happens most often—but not exclusively—during formal meditation practice.[48] Not exclusively, because knowledge can arise at any time given the right conditions. If a meditator's faculties are as sharp as Bāhiya's, it is possible to attain a high degree of insight or even enlightenment during daily activities. Here the stages of insight are not bypassed but experienced extremely rapidly in a few seconds. But in order to gain knowledge so quickly one would need to possess a large store of perfections[49] from previous lifetimes.

Bāhiya's instant enlightenment wasn't due to luck. In a previous existence he and some friends, taking only a few months' provisions, · scaled a mountain in order to practice meditation. Vowing to realize Nibbāna or die trying, they discarded their ladder so they couldn't climb down. Bāhiya died before glimpsing Nibbāna, but generated great spiritual aptitude from his strong resolution. This in part accounts for his rapid attainment when he met the Buddha.

During the Buddha's lifetime there were many others who reached awakening merely by hearing him preach. Yet because the level of mind is generally lower these days, most teachers agree that formal meditation practice is necessary if one aspires to Nibbāna.

* * *

---

48. Formal meditation is time devoted solely to vipassanā practice (whether sitting, walking, standing or lying down).

49. The perfections ("pāramitā") refer to an accumulation of wholesome qualities from past actions, performed either in the present life or in previous lifetimes. The ten perfections are: 1) generosity, 2) morality, 3) renunciation, 4) wisdom, 5) energy, 6) forbearance, 7) truthfulness, 8) resolution, 9) loving-kindness, 10) equanimity.

Although ultimate truth is closer than this page, it can't be seen until we drop the ordinary notions. But we don't need to throw them over the railing permanently. The Buddha didn't ask that we rashly abandon the mundane for the ultimate in one fell swoop; but he did urge us to stop mixing them up. Conventional truth is true in its own sphere. When dealing with the conventional, the Buddha said, it is appropriate to follow its rules. Yet even though wisdom gives a nod to the protocol it knows the deeper facts behind, like the stars behind a scattering of village lights.

Those who practice the Buddhist teachings should develop the flexibility of mind to switch from the ultimate perspective to the conventional, and vice-versa. Unfortunately, the inability to make this shift, even intellectually, is the cause of much misunderstanding and odd behavior among meditators. Most frequently misunderstood is the teaching of nonself or impersonality.

Nonself (*anattā*) means that what we term a living being is simply a temporary, changing aggregate of matter, consciousness and mental factors. Neither inside nor outside of this phenomenal stream can a self be found. These impersonal components cannot be manipulated as one wishes.

Truly speaking, we cannot choose what sights to see or sounds to hear. As we turn a corner the eye sees something ugly—it's too late to look away. Sometimes the ear hears the noise of hammering, or a motorcycle-engine, or a dog barking, even though we don't want to hear those sounds.

Who can snap his fingers and call up pleasant sights, sounds and flavors from thin air? Sometimes we can obtain them after making effort, but only because many conditions coincide with our desires, not because we can get those things merely by wanting.

As to the body: if our bones, cells and so on were Self, or truly belonged to a Self, we'd only have to think, "I want curly hair," and the hair would do our bidding. At the wish to be three inches taller or three sizes smaller—*presto!*—the corporeal frame would stretch or shrink accordingly.

Thoughts and feelings, as anyone who meditates knows, are just as wayward. They do not belong to us in the sense we cannot force them to be this way or that. If we try to have only good feelings, we will soon realize it can't be done.

Some people believe the teaching of nonselfness would leave us open to exploitation. But to realize anattā does not mean we'd relinquish our possessions to the first charlatan who came along, or allow someone to hurt us without trying to stop him. Those who truly understand anattā do not become foolish, passive or gullible.

Nonself does not mean the annihilation or destruction of the self. We cannot destroy that which never existed in the first place. Trying to do so would be absurd, like trying to bomb a fictional city.

A meditator's realization of anattā cannot be gauged by his level of involvement in society—whether he lives alone or with a large family, is a monastic or a householder, has few possessions or many. These outward signs are not a barometer for realization. Many householders in the Buddha's time attained awakening by contemplating nonself and later returned to family life.

However, if a person's understanding of anattā is genuine, he will not avoid ordinary responsibilities. A monk or nun has obligations just as a householder does. Aside from any other duties he is responsible for keeping the precepts and developing his mind, thereby making himself worthy of receiving alms. No matter what our obligations, a correct understanding of anattā does not lead to negligence. On the contrary, a person can fulfill his obligations more skillfully when there is less sense of ego to interfere.

One litmus test for the true understanding of nonself is to ask: has our burden of suffering decreased? Are we clinging less to pleasant sense-impressions? Insight into anattā, if genuine, invariably leads to decreased suffering. This is the natural result of diminished infatuation with sights, sounds, tastes and other sensations. Not that we have *aversion* to those sights and sounds. This point is often misunderstood. Aversion stems from hatred, a mental factor gradually eliminated through vipassanā practice. The correct practice of insight meditation cannot result in aversion.

But it's only natural, in seeing the emptiness and transience of both pleasant and unpleasant sensations, that a meditator's interest in them wanes. When our moods are no longer controlled by the hidden agendas of craving and aversion, we can be comfortable in almost any situation. The mind is then truly independent. There is nothing to be feared in this, no annihilation. It is not the self that is eliminated, only delusion. The person who sees nonself clearly grows *more* healthy and happy, rather than less so.

* * *

As long as we are living in the world, then, we should observe the social amenities. But within that framework there are many opportunities for knowing nāma or rūpa in the pure present. And when those chances arise—during an hour's meditation, for instance—the mind should sweep all conventions aside and let go. Of what? *Everything:* names, memories, expectations, preconceptions, feelings, judgments. As one teacher said, even let go of the idea of letting go. Then the mind, "won't even assume itself to be a mind or anything at all. In other words, it won't latch onto itself as being anything of any sort. All that remains is a pure condition of dhamma" (Kor Khao Suan Luang, *Looking Inward*, p. 3).

If we could truly drop the conventions, even a few moments would be enough. One second is all it takes to glimpse the truth, to reach a level of wisdom. Afterwards, consciousness returns to conventional perception; but the mind doesn't forget what it saw. Having once spotted the picture up close it can never view the daily scenes in quite the same way.

But if we try to know real phenomena through concepts, as if the former were a kind of fractal of the latter, we'll end up twisting things because the two are different at every point, just as a photographic negative is the converse, point for point, of its print. Or it would be like mixing our daily conventions with the particle-world, expecting, say, the protons in a dinner plate to look like tiny saucers. On the physical level we accept that beings and objects dissolve into particles, mere gusts of probability, their conventional features untraceable. One wouldn't expect to find mice or men at the quantum level. Likewise, it behooves us not to keep peering under rocks asking, "Where have all the people gone?" when approaching ultimate truth.

Some have suggested that Just Seeing a man or a woman means to perceive muscle, skin and bones only. To be sure, this is more in line with absolute reality than beholding a Being endowed with a self. But in the end one must go further, because those body parts are still concepts, only lower down the conceptual ladder than the idea of a person. "When you see the bones of people," Achan Kor wrote, "your perception labels them: 'That's a person's skeleton. That's a person's skull' ... Actually, there are no bones at all ... You have to penetrate into the bones so that they're elements. Otherwise you'll get stuck at the level of skeleton ... This shows that you haven't penetrated into the dhamma. You're stuck at the outer shell."[50]

Why are muscle, skin and bone still at the "outer shell"? We envision a muscle as something that can be seen and touched both. But in the ultimate sense, a genuine material form can only be experienced through one of the five sense-doors. A smell cannot be seen; a sound cannot be smelled; a taste cannot be heard.[51] If we believe that something can be seen and touched, that object is not an ultimate reality but a concept. As Ven. Kapilavaddho pointed out, you cannot touch what you see.

In the *ultimate* sense, anything we love or hate, whether object or living being (including ourselves), can ultimately be dissected into momentary units of color, sound, smell, taste, tactile form, consciousness, and mental factors, with nothing left over. Every one of these blips is impersonal. What we call a "man" or a "woman" is only a composite of separate phenomena experienced over time in different moments. Memory connects the dots, building a mental formation.

Even when looking at our spouse we see only color—but the mind sculpts the hue into three dimensions, augmenting the bare rūpa with descriptions of raven hair or sea-green eyes. In addition to images we experience sound, which is labeled as the loved one's voice. But sound vibrations are impersonal. They don't belong to a Dave or a Mary. Then there is touch; but in truth we cannot touch the dear one's hand. We touch only rūpa, material form made of earth, air, water and fire. Those elements, being subject to their own natural laws, can't be made into ego's property. How could we physically touch a *self*?

Moments of seeing, hearing and touching seem to occur at the same time. But if we could slow the perceptual movie we'd know they are not simultaneous. In one moment, for instance, we cannot both hear and see a flock of pigeons. Seeing and hearing are

---

50. Kor Khao Suan Luang, *Reading the Mind*, p. 24. On the difference between vipassanā and meditation practices that do not go beyond muscles and bones, see Mahāsi Sayādaw, *Discourse on Hemavata Sutta*, p. 95.
51. Conceptual objects are only experienced through the mind-door. Each of the five sense-impressions can be experienced through two doors, their respective sense-door and the mind-door.

discrete events that flare up one at a time, in rapid succession. It's only because these perceptions rush by so fast that whole groups of phenomena seem to land at once.

In conventional perception, color, sound, scent, tactile form and flavor seem to be different aspects of a single object, not separate objects in their own rights. Suppose we are holding a gardenia flower, touching the waxy petals and smelling the fragrance. The mysterious scent and the softness the fingers sense both belong to, or come from, one object: the flower. Or that's what we assume. Reasoning back from the scent we arrive at the blossom as the origin—the root, as it were, from which the perfume sprung. But isn't it backward to dub a blossom a root?

In absolute terms, scent and softness come first. These bare sense-impressions are the more primal entities, ultimately real. They are not created in the mind. The idea of a Thing that embraces both scent and softness comes after and is learned. Yet if the flower comes after, how could it be the source of the scent and softness? On the contrary, the concept "gardenia" is fashioned from *them*.

Normally, the mind, in a quick perceptual maneuver, connects the dots of scent and softness, dubbing the whole thing "gardenia." But having drawn an unbroken line through what are actually separate sensations, the mind is hoist by its own petard, believing the creation to have an identity that is objectively real, and eventually suffering because of that belief.

But when viewed from the ultimate standpoint, the single conventional Thing *gardenia* "splinters" into several different rūpas. Whereas in normal perception we experience one object, the flower, in ultimate terms we experience two, scent and touch; three if we add the rūpa of color.

Tracing the fragrance and softness back to their origins, we find that their causal lines do not converge in a blossom. They don't converge in anything else, either, because these two sense-impressions don't share a common origin. (The same is true of color, sound and taste). The fragrance arises from a different cluster of causes than does the softness, even though, in normal thought and speech, we lump them together as belonging to a flower.

Each kind of sense-impression, furthermore, approaches awareness through a different perceptual door. Through which entrance could a gardenia be known? Through the nose? Only fragrance, not a flower, is sensed through the nose. Through the hands? Only softness or hardness is experienced through the tactile sense. Through the eyes? The cream and green tint that contacts the eye is only visible form. There is, in fact, no physical sense-door through which a gardenia could enter, because it is a mental construct, not a physical phenomenon.

Ultimately speaking, a gardenia is a concept that results when the mind strings several memories together—memories of separate sensations. Or we could view it as a temporal bridge seeming to span the gap between scent, color and touch. Although we usually don't notice the breaks in our experience, don't see the cessation between moments of scent and touch, the gap is still there. It can be seen by those who cultivate mindfulness.

Likewise, in perceiving a person the mind drags its net across memory, gathering the echoes of past phenomena, pulling them together in a single catch. But the result is only a mental formation rather than a genuine entity. The same is true of the concept called "I."

* * *

And yet, even when it is seen that no selves exist in ultimate terms, we should not forget, in the conventional sense, the world is filled with individual beings, all of whom desire happiness as much as we do. In the end neither view, whether ultimate or conventional, should be clung to.

Once, during a meditation retreat, a student came to Achan Sobin in great distress saying, "I don't exist."

Achan Sobin smiled and pointed to her legs. "What are those?" He asked.

"They're legs," she said.

"And what are these?" He asked, pointing to her hands.

"Hands."

"Yes, hands and legs … In the ordinary sense, you can touch them, can't you? Even though you begin to see that your self does not exist according to ultimate reality, it still exists in the conventional sense, or how could you live in the world? You eat, you sleep, you walk. Truth is like the hand." He showed her the back of his hand. "This side is conventional truth. The other side," he said, turning his hand over to show the palm, "is ultimate truth.

Just the underside of the same thing."[52] We might add, while conventional and ultimate truth both exist, the conventional is true only relatively, whereas the ultimate is true absolutely.

It is especially important to separate ultimate facts from the sphere of ordinary morality, which pertains to the conventional world. Failing to do so may lead to morally irresponsible or dangerous views. "There must," Mahāsi Sayādaw remarks, "be no encroachment from one area to another, for instance, from the area of wisdom to the area of morality."[53]

The Buddha never implied that those who perceive ultimate truth, ceasing to cling to conventions and concepts, are above moral strictures and can do whatever they like. Unfortunately, some individuals, lacking personal experience of the dhamma, would distort the higher teachings to justify their own wrong behavior.

As Mahāsi Sayādaw explains in *A Discourse on Hemavata Sutta*, some people argue there is no moral difference between cutting a chicken and cutting a piece of wood, since both are comprised of elemental matter. This is clearly against the Buddha's doctrine, since the Buddha espoused morality as a necessary foundation for wisdom. In the Buddha's time a bhikkhu named Arittha argued that monks, who take vows of celibacy, ought to be allowed sexual contact with women because, ultimately speaking, there is no difference between touching a woman and touching a robe. While it is true there is no difference in the ultimate sense, there *is* a difference conventionally, which allows for a tremendous moral difference. "Such sophistry is terrifying," Mahāsi Sayādaw writes; "... those who rely on such teachers are in for moral disaster."[54]

The dhamma, when wrongly grasped, becomes dangerous. The Buddha compared it to lifting a poisonous snake by the tail instead of the neck. When held by the tail it can swing around to bite you.

---

52. Personal communication with the author. In regard to anxiety about ceasing to exist, see *Majjhima Nikāya* 22.
53. *Discourse on Hemavata Sutta*, p. 96.
54. *Sallekha Sutta*, p. 273.

CHAPTER 5

The sky is dark behind the mountains now. With a hum the porch light clicks on, lighting the poplars in the yard. Their branches, pitching in the wind, stipple a board fence with shadow. Will it rain again, the mind wonders? No—the clouds have cleared. *There in the sky*—a falling spark. Another and another—*meteor shower.* Down the long drive a trashcan is rolling, clattering loudly, past all the poplars. Movement leaps up everywhere the eye looks, in sky, yard—movement of leaf, shadow and star.

At the edge of the lawn, heads of pale cosmos bob above a crosshatch of stems. Those stems are hollow pipes, as hollow as the trunk of a plantain-tree. "Formations are like a plantain-trunk," the Buddha said; empty, lacking substance. "Form is a lump of foam, feeling a bubble; perception a mirage, and consciousness a conjuring-trick" (SN 22:95).

Perception is a mirage. Shadows sweep across weathered boards; through the mind swings the shadow of doubt. Could it be, the thought comes (the tossing leaves seen somewhat differently now), that all this movement—the shifting patterns on the slats, the branches, the rolling garbage can—could it be that all this visual movement is a mirage, too?

We don't need the Buddha's teachings to know that visual perception can be deceptive. It is this potential for deception that is exploited in magic tricks and sleight-of-hand con games. A deception can be innocent, too. For instance a heavy glass vase, as we lift it, might fly up in the hand because we overestimated the weight. It looked like glass but is really plastic.

A hologram-rose looks uncannily real. Though we may know it's an intangible image made by lasers, put it next to a real rose and the mind does back flips trying to tell the difference. A burner on the stove looks hot, but we can't actually *see* heat. We merely infer from previous experience that when a burner glows red our fingers could blister. "Solidity, heat and motion," Mahāsi Sayādaw explains, can be known only by touching … It is a popular belief that we can identify the primary elements by seeing. A rock or an iron bar looks hard, no doubt, but this is not due to seeing. It is just an inference based on past experience. What we know by seeing is only the appearance, which sometimes gives a false impression. This is evident when we tread on what looks like solid ground and stumble into a quagmire, or when we get burnt by unwittingly handling a hot iron bar. (*Dependent Origination*, pp. 80–1)

It is one thing to accept that we cannot see weight and heat. These perceptions, most of us know, are based on inferences grown automatic through habit. But *motion itself*? All day long we seem to perceive movement with our eyes, including the movement of our own bodies. When brushing the teeth, for example, we see the hand move up and down. The wrist circles as we stir our tea, the legs pump in exercise class, the fingers tap the keyboard. That's to say nothing of the movement of beings and objects outside of ourselves. The conviction that every day we see things run, fall, glide, jump, spin and otherwise move seems to be hard-wired into the brain. "And yet", the Sayādaw continues, "We know that an object is moving because we see it first here and then there, but its motion is only inferred" (ibid., p. 81).

In regard to the question of visual motion, Mahāsi Sayādaw tells the following story: Once there was a layman who shook a pillow in front of a monk, asking what elements (*dhammas*) he saw passing away.

The bhikkhu replied, "'I see the element of motion passing away.'

'Venerable sir,'" said the layman, "'… if you are mindful at the moment of seeing, you can know only what happens to the visual form. You cannot know anything empirically about the element of motion at that moment. Insight meditation gives priority to what can be known directly. The element of motion can be known only through body-contact'" (ibid.).

But if ultimate realities (including visual forms) arise and vanish, doesn't that mean we can see them moving? We can, by means of insight, see realities appear and pass away in a single moment. But since an ultimate form arises and winks out *instantly,* there is no time for it to move over to another place before dying out.

Chapter 5

In normal perception, Mahāsi Sayādaw explains, a man
walking toward us appears as a single shape advancing from point
A to point B. It seems there is only one form—the same one—
moving from one spot to another. But when insight is well-
developed, we may see a succession of separate forms arising and
passing away when watching a person or object approach. Each
one is seen to vanish at the spot where it arose.[55]

To get some idea of this, imagine a series of fireworks being
shot off like a line of dominoes. As soon as one burst dies out, the
next one goes off down the line. Let's say that each firework is
shaped like a dragon. To someone watching from a distance, it
would look as if a dragon of light were flying south. But each
firework dies out right where it detonates.

Or think of an animated film sequence. In each frame the
cartoon figure is stationary. But if we alter its position slightly in
every successive frame, we can give the effect of a person riding
into the sunset or running toward a precipice.

The meditator with strong insight knows, "Absolute realities
do not move over to another place; material forms from afar do not
come near; material forms which are near do not go afar. They
cease and vanish at the place where they come into existence. They
are, therefore, impermanent, suffering and not self" (Mahāsi
Sayādaw, Great Discourse, p. 130).[56]

* * *

The Buddha said that we should know the eye. There seems to be
a live camera inside us, this eye contiguous with this I. But the
corporeal orb is only a physical mechanism—unconscious,
incurious. The eye has no desire to eye. It's the mind that wants to see.

---

55. As the Sayādaw describes it, "While looking at a man approaching
from a distance, and noting, 'seeing, seeing,' we see him disappearing
part by part in a series of quick, blurring fade-outs". Great Discourse, p. 129.
56. In Fundamentals of Insight Mahāsi Sayādaw explains, "Ordinary people
think it is the same hand that moves, that has existed before the bending,
and that will exist after the bending. To them it is ever unchanging. This is
because they fail to penetrate the way matter arises in succession.
Impermanence is said to be hidden by continuity. It is hidden because one
does not meditate on what arises and passes away" (p. 35).

"Dependent on eye and visible forms, eye-consciousness (seeing) arises; the coincidence of the three is contact" (SN 12:43). Who can stop sound from arising when a drum is struck? Does the sound care if we want it to arise? Sound-waves issue forth as a matter of course when the stick contacts the drum. Likewise, seeing is inevitable when the right conditions come together, namely: a functioning eye, a visible object, light, and attention, which must occur simultaneously. Because we are seeing this page (conventionally speaking), we know those conditions are present now.

To understand the eye is to know it is not an extension of the ego. "And what," the Buddha asked, "is void of self and self's property? The eye ... forms ... eye-consciousness ... [are] void of self and self's property" (SN 35:85). Our eyes do not share our desires, let alone follow them. Instead they go their own way according to natural, physical laws. For that reason they can't be regarded as self, or as something belonging to a self.

The same is true of visual forms: Color-patches don't hasten to appear because we want to see them or obligingly vanish when we don't. They're indifferent to our wishes.

The last term in the triad, consciousness, is the most difficult to understand because it seems closest to us—seems, in fact, identical to us. But even the consciousness that sees does not follow our desires. Sometimes we might want to see and yet be unable to: Perhaps the electricity goes out and we have no candles, or the eyes fail to function due to illness or accident. Seeing-consciousness can't arise then, no matter how hard we try to induce it. It is impossible to manufacture sense-perception at will, out of the grist of desire.

In truth, every act of visual perception occurs without a doer. Within the triad of eye, image and eye-consciousness, no manager can be found, no Self who sits in the control-booth turning the dials of the process. There is no seer, just the seeing; no hearer, just the hearing. The same is true of smelling, tasting, touching and even thinking.

Like the meteors sparking and dying out above the mountains, the particles of matter in the physical eye are momentary, forming and perishing every second. For that reason, "if one says, 'the eye is self,' it is just like saying one's self is arising and passing away, not stable. Therefore, it must be concluded that the unenduring material quality of the eye is not self" (Mahāsi Sayādaw, *Great Discourse*, p. 83). The same is true of images themselves. When a meditator Just Sees color he knows it as rūpa, an unstable rush of sensation that he cannot grasp or control. As the Buddha said:

> Eye-contact is impermanent, changing, its state is 'becoming otherness' ... This eye-contact, arising as it does from an impermanent relation—how could it be permanent? Contacted, monks, one feels. Contacted, one intends. Contacted, one perceives. Thus these states also are mobile and transitory, impermanent and changing. (SN 35:93)

It is not only the physical eye and images, but also the mental components of seeing that are always in the process of becoming-otherness. As soon as we see a color-patch, that cognitive event, with its attendant feelings and mental qualities, sputters out. Nothing about it can be pinned down and stabilized. "The perceptions which recognized sense objects a moment ago", said Mahāsi Sayādaw, "do not reach the present moment; they disappeared even while recognizing.... The perceptions which are recognizing and remembering things now also perish while actually recognizing.... The perceptions which will recognize things in the future will also vanish at the time of recognizing and they are therefore impermanent, suffering and not self" (*Great Discourse*, p. 137).

What can be found, in any given moment, aside from these shifting aggregates: matter, feeling, perception, mental formations and consciousness? In the end this is all we are—empty bursts of phosphorescence.

But even if these sobering facts are true (or because they are true), how does it help to be aware of them? If everything is indeed impersonal, fleeting, and slipping out of reach, what can be gained by Just Seeing, Hearing, and Knowing?

Just Seeing could be regarded as the ultimate form of sense restraint. As part of the training in morality we exercise moderation in daily life, not allowing ourselves to cling to pleasant sensations to the point of obsession. By keeping watch at the sense-doors, we prevent the thirst for pleasant color, sound, smell, flavor and touch from growing stronger. Intense desire always involves suffering, since the longing itself is unpleasant and agitating.

Eventually, as insight becomes subtle and sharp through vipassanā practice, we will be able to keep the mind in a state of equanimity, protected from the pain of attachment, no matter what kinds of objects are coming in through the sense-doors.

In comparing this independence to the frantic involvement in pleasure, it will be obvious that the ease of nonattachment is superior, and we will be moved to cut away more and more entanglements. When it finally hits home that sense-impressions *really* cannot be owned or controlled, the naïve infatuation with them fades. Then there is nothing to do but let go.

In letting go we don't lose any happiness. On the contrary, we find it. Suffering diminishes drastically when the mind stops trying to grasp what is only a shimmer of spray. What arises in its place, the suttas tell us, is genuine happiness of an entirely different order, characterized by freedom. We begin to know an ease that doesn't fluctuate with the pull of light and dark events. As Achan Sobin remarks, "First you take care of mindfulness, then mindfulness will take care of you."

We might ask ourselves: Can something be thought desirable that lasts barely long enough to be focused on? "In fact [mind and matter] seem to vanish every time one takes a close look at them," Ven. Sujīva writes. "They disappear so fast they don't seem to be there at all! ... Such experiences finally culminate in total detachment, realization of suffering *and its cessation*" (*Wisdom Treasury,* p. 8. Italics added). The permanent uprooting of suffering—any and every kind of distress we can name—is the ultimate benefit of Just Seeing.

Ceasing to be overcome by forms, we will overcome *them*:

> And how, friends, is one free from lust? Herein, friends, a monk, seeing an object with the eye, is not attached to objects that charm, nor averse to objects that displease ... but dwells, having established mindfulness of the body and his thought is boundless. So that he realizes in its true nature that emancipation of heart, that emancipation of wisdom ... Moreover, friends, so dwelling a monk conquers (visible) objects, objects do not conquer him. (SN 35:202)

There is nothing more worth trying to conquer, because in conquering objects we conquer dukkha.

CHAPTER 6

How can we shift our perspective from the conventional to the ultimate? How can we learn to Just See, Hear and Know? Not by willpower alone. Someone who has never touched a piano couldn't will himself to play a Chopin waltz. Seeing forms as the Buddha did, with the eye of wisdom, depends not on willpower but on creating the right conditions. We can generate those conditions by training the mind in vipassanā.

This training is within reach of everyone. A remote forest or cave is not required. Insight meditation can be practiced in any reasonably quiet place—a room in our house, a garden or even the office at break-time. But in order to get results we should meditate daily. As musical skill results from hours of practicing an instrument, Just Seeing results from the ongoing cultivation of wise attention (*yoniso manasikāra*), mindfulness (*sati*), and clear comprehension (*sampajanna*). The aim is to produce a few moments of supramundane wisdom.

How do these factors—wise attention, mindfulness, clear comprehension and wisdom—differ? Before the invention of lighters and matches, fire was only obtained by effort—the effort of rubbing dry sticks together. As Achan Sobin explains, a meditator wants to generate fire, the fire of wisdom. His sticks are nāma (mind) and rūpa (matter). His job is to observe them continuously, from moment to moment.

Wise attention keeps his mind on the task and knows if he's "moving the sticks" too slowly or not. After a time the friction generates heat. Such weak heat can't transform anything yet—it can't boil water or fry a fish. The heat is analogous to clear comprehension, which could be called the beginning of insight-knowledge (*vipassanā-nana*). But this level of insight isn't yet strong enough to burn off the greed, hatred and delusion in the mind.

As the student continues the work of noticing objects, there comes a moment when he clearly sees impermanence, suffering, or nonself in a single instance of nāma-rūpa. (This is like smelling the smoke from the sticks). It is wisdom that understands these characteristics, but this wisdom is still of the mundane sphere.

Eventually, many wholesome factors harmonize in a fire that consumes the fetters, transforming the student from an ordinary being to a Noble One.[57] With this experience the student attains supramundane wisdom. In practice, wise attention, mindfulness, and the rest are difficult to separate because they work together. Let's take a closer look at these factors, in the context of a meditation retreat.

As we said, vipassanā may be practiced at home for thirty minutes or more daily. Some meditators also practice for extended periods called "retreats," the length of which ranges from one day to several months. During that time the student gives up outside concerns and devotes the entire day to meditation. All physical activities are slowed down. Even when eating, bathing or brushing his teeth he maintains as much attention to the present moment as possible. His only concern is cultivating mindfulness and its supporting qualities.

Mindfulness, in vipassanā practice, is the faculty that is aware of whatever object appears in the present moment. Like a camera, which does not evaluate the picture it takes, mindfulness merely registers the form. It does not describe, reflect upon, or verbalize about the object. Mindfulness does not mean *thinking* about sense-impressions, but merely knowing them with bare attention.

As a baby needs a walker, a fledgling mindfulness needs the support of momentary concentration. Although not as strong as the concentration (*samādhi*) developed in tranquility practice, momentary concentration is sufficient for vipassanā because it effectively suppresses the five mental hindrances: lust, ill-will, sleepiness, restlessness, and doubt. "It is possible," Mahāsi Sayādaw remarks, "to begin straightaway with insight meditation without having previously developed full concentration in jhāna."[58] (In "jhāna," awareness of the five sense-impressions is

---

57. Enlightened beings are referred to as Noble Ones. (Enlightenment, *bodhi*, means to awaken from ignorance.) The four kinds of Noble persons are: the streamwinner (*sotāpanna*), the once-returner, (*sakadāgāmi*), the non-returner (*anāgāmi*) and the holy one (*arahant*). At each stage a deeper level of fetters is destroyed.

58. *Practical Insight*, p. 58. For arguments in support of this view see Mahāsi Sayādaw, ibid., pp. 58–62, and *Progress of Insight*, pp. 6–8; and Nyanaponika, *Heart of Buddhist Meditation*, pp. 114–17.

suspended, but the mind is fully conscious.)

Momentary concentration prevents the mind from drifting off the meditation object. Although a certain degree of samādhi is essential, an excess in the early stages can slow progress. The beginning student aims to balance mindfulness and concentration by developing them at an equal rate. In the early stages of practice these two factors must be adjusted until the objects of awareness grow clear, like adjusting two binocular lenses until the image jumps into focus.

Wise attention (*yoniso manasikāra*) reminds the meditator to keep noting objects in the present moment only. When the meditator notices the mind wandering, wise attention brings him back to the principal object. It is the voice that tells him not to follow desire or hatred. If the meditator smells food and thinks, "I'm hungry! How long till lunch?" wise attention checks the rush of liking, preventing desire from increasing. If a stab of pain makes aversion arise, *yoniso manasikāra* reminds the student to observe the pain before shifting the body.

The mind, in the early stages of training, often dwells on memories or rushes forward in a tangle of plans; but neither memory nor fantasy is a present-moment object. In order to keep his awareness steady, the beginner labels phenomena with a mental note. (This technique is only a temporary crutch. The mental notes should be dropped when clear comprehension and mindfulness are strong enough.)

A mental note—also called a "label"—is a word or short phrase said silently in the mind at the same time you notice an object. It describes the object in general but not in detail. For example, when hearing a sound you would note "hearing," instead of "dog barking." If an unpleasant sensation arose you would note "pain" or "feeling" instead of "sharp pain in my knee."

A mental note should be limited to one or two words. If it's too long another object will have arisen by the time you finish saying the note. It should also be a word easily recalled so you don't have to search your mind for it. Labeling an object with a mental note in vipassanā training should not be confused with knowing the conventional name of an object. The former helps support mindfulness in the early stages, leading to the growth of insight.

Mental notes help you keep track of sense-impressions as they appear so that nothing is missed. They help prevent the arising of aversion when you feel pain, desire when you feel pleasure, and delusion when the object is neutral. But as soon as an object is noted it should be let go. Even the sensation or thought you noted one moment before should not be kept in the mind. Every phenomenon should be forgotten as soon as it is noticed.

The basic meditation method is to observe the abdominal motions that occur during respiration. As you inhale, the abdomen expands. That movement is called "rising." As you exhale, the abdomen contracts. That's called "falling." The meditator labels the movement silently as he watches it, noting, "rising, falling, rising, falling."

The meditator notices only what is occurring in the *immediate present*. To continue to think about the falling motion when the abdomen has already begun to rise is to stray into the past, to remember an object that is already gone. When the abdomen is rising, where is the falling motion? Can it be found? It cannot, since it no longer exists. It is now only a memory, not a real object in the immediate present. After a second or two the inhalation ends and a new exhalation occurs. Now the rising motion is in the past and the falling movement is the present object. This new instance of falling is not identical to any of the falling motions that happened before. It is not the same phenomenon cycling into view again, but an entirely new event being born.

Truly speaking, the rising-falling motions do not constitute a continuous loop. The abdomen must stop rising for a split second before it begins to fall. Likewise, it must stop falling before rising again. Each instance of rising or falling is a discrete event. As Achan Sobin explains, the last breath is in the past. The next breath hasn't happened yet. Only the present breath (or sight, sound, etc.) is real; only this is actually happening *now*.

Sooner or later the student will forget to watch the movement and begin to think about something. When the mind wanders away he should note "thinking," saying the word mentally, and then resume noting the abdominal movements.

Although the rising-falling motions constitute the primary object, the meditator's focus isn't exclusively on them. Every phenomenon should be noticed. When an itch appears, the student notes "itching." When he's aware of a scent he notes "smelling."

On hearing a sound, he notes "hearing." When a feeling of pain or pleasure appears he notes "pain," "pleasure," or "feeling." When confused, he notes "confusion." No matter what mental or physical phenomenon arises, the meditator knows it and lets it go.

During an intensive retreat a student alternates the basic exercise—observing the abdominal motions—with equal time spent practicing walking meditation. While walking he ignores the rising-falling movements and focuses only on the movement of the foot.

There are a few techniques for developing insight more quickly. One strategy is to drop the feeling of "I" as much as possible and simply know the phenomenal experience of the present moment. Rather than thinking: *"I am feeling," "I am hearing," "I am moving,"* simply know: *feeling, hearing, moving.* If there's a cramp in your leg, for example, label the sensation with the mental note "pain" or "feeling," without regarding it as "me" or mentally linking it to a body part.

Instead of identifying the objects being noted (or the act of knowing them) with the ego, pull your attention back. Observe the mind-body process as if it were a specimen under a microscope, having nothing to do with your self. The false belief in self can't be willed away; but as you cease to reinforce it you will see, in intermittent glimpses, that your moment-to-moment experience is only a series of impersonal sensations known by an impersonal mind.

It is important to focus on one object, i.e., one sense-datum, at a time. Observing two sense-impressions together scatters and slows awareness. Instead of attending to the whole stream of experience at once, the student, while watching the abdominal motions, pays no attention to sounds, sights or smells. When noting hearing he ignores the objects from the other senses. When chewing, he observes only taste or the movement of the jaw.

Not that he observes one kind of object exclusively for an hour; but he knows only one object *per moment.* If a loud sound distracts him from the rising-falling motions, he switches his attention to the sound and notes "hearing" for a few moments, then returns to observing the abdominal movements. When noting hearing he pays no attention to the stomach's motion. The same procedure applies to all sensations—smells, thoughts, itches, emotions, pain and so on.

Experience becomes a series of separate moments like beads on a string, each moment containing a single object. By focusing on one sense-datum at a time, the student is able to perceive the three phases of each moment—arising, persisting, and vanishing—more and more clearly.

On the other hand, if a beginner tries to be aware in a general way of whatever comes up, noticing is vague. Because his attention is scattered across several objects at once, none is particularly clear. Since he is trying to observe the whole stream of experience simultaneously, he may not know which object he's noting at any given moment. In that case it's difficult to see the arising and passing away of any one segment of the stream. But when focusing on one drop at a time, so to speak, he is able to track that phenomenon from its birth to its dissolution. When two or more objects occur simultaneously—a movement and a sound, say—he should observe the more vivid one, or the one that triggers more craving or hatred.

In vipassanā the way of focusing on objects differs from that of concentration practice, and we need a way of describing the difference. Looking around the room for inspiration, our eyes land again on Seurat's *Island*. This painting has taught us much already. On the left side of the canvas sits the man in the top hat, gazing at the river. We imagine him swinging his cane as he follows the progress of the boats and then stopping, mesmerized, to watch the sticks of light that gather and splinter on the water.

Strangely, in the midst of this reverie, three yellow dots seem to drop from the painting onto the wood floor, bouncing as they land. (What kind of daydream is this?) Then something else: our man from the painting drops his cane and steps awkwardly out of the canvas, one leg at a time, like a thief coming in through a window. After scanning the hall he brushes the dust from his sleeves, sweeps off his hat, bows in our direction, and commences to juggle the three yellow dots, now the size of golf balls. A moment later he stops juggling, staring at us without a word. What is it that we are supposed to understand? Of course. Some mental lever clicks. Here is our example.

A juggler's focus, like that in vipassanā, is touch-and-go. "Focus and forget it" is the motto. The student must follow both halves of the maxim if he wants to get maximum benefit from practice. As to the first half: the juggler must focus in order to catch the ball. He must know where to put his attention and then keep his mind on that spot. With the next ball coming toward him, he can't think about the last. He'll fail if he's distracted by a noise or his gaze drifts away.

The meditator, too, must keep his attention in the present moment or he'll drop the ball—miss the now and observe an object that has already passed. As we said before, each moment consists of three phases: arising, persisting, and vanishing. To observe one rise of the abdomen takes about two or three seconds (since that's how long one rising movement lasts). Ideally the attention should be equally alert throughout this arc, for the entire duration of the movement. It isn't enough just to notice the development in the middle. The beginning- and end-points should be noticed, too. But one shouldn't mentally chop the movement into sections. The whole motion should be noticed smoothly, without break. The same should be done when the abdomen falls, the foot moves forward, and so on.

Now for the "forget it" part: as soon as the juggler catches a ball he lets it go—otherwise how could he catch the next one? His attention doesn't stick. He keeps it moving, jumping from one object to the next. What kind of performer would pause to gaze at the ball he'd just caught, unwilling to surrender it because he liked the color? Likewise, as soon the meditator notes an object he should drop it, or he won't be able to catch the *next* phenomenon. His attention should rest no longer than one moment on any form. For example, after observing one rising movement from start to finish, he should let it go.

If the same object—a sound, say—appears again after being noted once, the student observes it a second time, then lets it go again, and so on. He notes, "hearing ... hearing ... hearing ..." in a sequence of moments, letting go after each one. But now red flags are springing up, for this is a subtle and important point, one to be taken to heart.

It would be easy to assume that observing the same object repeatedly does not differ from concentration practice, in which uninterrupted attention is fixed on a single object. But in fact these are very different techniques. Observing a thing repeatedly, one separate moment after another, is worlds away from keeping the mind seamlessly *fixed* on that object. In the first case the student can see the mind moving as he re-focuses on the object. In concentration practice he cannot. In vipassanā he notes the object for one moment, drops it, then observes the same form if it appears again. The experience is of a series of separate moments, each one arising and passing away in succession.[59] In concentration practice, on the other hand, one doesn't release the object at the end of each moment but keeps hanging on. Perceiving no movement, it seems that time has stopped.

Mind and matter are ever-changing. Nothing that's conditioned can be still, even for a second. To keep up with the flux, the student drops the old object in order to catch the next thing rising up in the present, even if it's the "same" thing he noted one moment before. The motto is: know—and let go. We have to let go to keep pace with the changing present.

Another strategy, especially important during a retreat, is to maintain continuity of practice. A single day of continuous mindfulness is worth more than seven days' interrupted meditation. "Continuous" does not refer to the number of hours we sit in formal meditation. It means to maintain uninterrupted awareness in whatever we do.

This can be seen, for instance, in the way a student changes posture. A conscientious meditator does not stand up abruptly or carelessly stretch as soon as the sitting period is over. Before changing position he observes the intention to move. He then maintains moment-to-moment awareness during the transition from sitting to standing, breaking the entire physical action into a series of small, discrete movements. The same procedure applies when he stops walking and returns to sitting meditation. During an intensive retreat a student moves mindfully and slowly at all times unless the nature of the action prevents it (splashing water on the face, for instance, can't be done slowly). Throughout the day he notes every physical action whenever changing posture, eating,

---

59. For the vipassanā student, Mahāsi Sayādaw writes, "A pleasant sight vanishes as soon as it is noted. But since there is [still] eye and visual object, the sight is seen again. Every time it is seen, it is noted and quickly vanishes." *Great Discourse*, p. 71. The same occurs with unpleasant and neutral objects.

using the bathroom, getting into bed at night, and so on. (Again, we are speaking of a retreat. In ordinary life it isn't practical to note every action in a step-by-step manner.)

It is important to observe the intention to move before actually shifting the body. This technique can be applied to any activity. Before extending the hand to grasp a cup, for instance, one should note the flare of wanting that triggers the physical impulse. By noticing our intentions we come to see firsthand how fetters such as craving are ignited from contact with objects.

As we said earlier, there are sixteen stages of insight-knowledge, which we shall describe here.[60] But the reader should be cautioned that learning about these insights beforehand might cause him to anticipate results, thereby slowing his progress. For that reason, Mahāsi Sayādaw writes, "It is not good for a pupil who meditates under the guidance of a teacher to get acquainted with these stages before meditation begins" (*Practical Insight*, p. 35). Meditators with access to a teacher should skip to Chapter Seven. The following descriptions are intended for those students without an instructor, or those who have already reached a fairly advanced stage of insight.

Knowledge is either conceptual or practical. Since these descriptions fall under the first category, they should not be taken as infallible guides. Not all meditators will undergo every experience described here,[61] and many things may happen that are not listed.

The student should not try to make his experience fit into a preconceived scheme. The mind can play all kinds of tricks. Having read about an experience, the subconscious mind may try to fabricate it. Although such illusions are only mental formations, the meditator himself may not be able to distinguish the trick from the genuine article.

---

60. For more on the sixteen stages of insight, see http://www.vipassanadhura.com/sixteen.htm.
61. Although all meditators must pass through every level of insight, the stages may be accompanied by different unusual experiences, not all of which happen to every student. Furthermore, some meditators have no clear view of certain stages because they pass them so quickly. See *Practical Insight*, p. 41.

If pride develops when a meditator reaches a stage of insight, that pride should be noted. On the other hand, the student should not get discouraged if he hasn't progressed very far. Discouragement, too, should be noted when it appears. The intelligent meditator will avoid getting caught up in emotional reactions. He only has to keep following the right path and progress will result as a matter of course.

In spite of the potential drawbacks, learning about the stages of insight can inspire confidence by their very predictability. A meditator's faith in the path increases when he begins to experience some of the things he has read about. "The first four levels happened as they said," he thinks, "so maybe the others will, too."

Theoretical knowledge can sometimes help a meditator avoid getting stuck. Prior knowledge of the so-called "imperfections of insight," for example, might prevent a student from clinging to those states. The traps of elation, disappointment and self-deception can be avoided if the meditator uses this information intelligently, with continuous self-examination and scrupulous honesty.

Now let's turn to the stages of insight themselves. At the first level of vipassanā, the student realizes that nāma, mind, is distinct from rūpa, matter. All day long we breathe in and out. Normally we experience the abdominal movements and the act of knowing them as a seamless happening bound up with the concept "me." These factors seem melded together, indistinguishable one from another. As Mahāsi Sayādaw tells us,

> The material form and the mind that notes it ... seem to be one and the same thing. Your book knowledge may tell you that they are separate, but your personal experience knows them as one thing. Shake your index finger. Do you see the mind that intends to shake? Can you distinguish between the mind and the shaking? If you are sincere, the answer will be "no."[62]

But at the first stage of insight the meditator's experience, "begins to appear to him as consisting of two functionally distinguishable parts—mind and matter—rather than as a single unit."[63] He knows, for example, that the abdominal motion is one

---

62. *Fundamentals of Insight*, p. 29.
63. Mahāthera Matara Sri Ñāṇārāma, *Seven Stages of Purification*, p. 19.

thing (rūpa) and the knowing of it another (nāma).

This applies to any object perceived, not only the abdominal movements. When looking at an image the student knows that the eye and color are material (rūpa), whereas the act of seeing is a mental event (nāma). The same holds true for the ear, nose, tongue, body, their corresponding objects, and the act of knowing them. "To the meditator whose mindfulness and concentration are well-developed", says Mahāsi Sayādaw, "the object of attention and the awareness of it are as separate as a wall and a stone that is thrown at it".[64] This knowledge is so important that Achan Sobin once remarked, "There is no vipassanā without nāma and rūpa".

At the second level of insight, the meditator understands the causal relationship between mind and matter. Sometimes the mind functions as cause, sometimes matter. The body cannot move by itself; the intention to move must occur first. When you lift your foot the mind is the cause, the body's movement (materiality) the effect. On the other hand, when tasting a flavor the thought may arise, "Delicious! I want to have more." In that case materiality (the flavor) is the cause and mentality (the thought) the effect.

On reaching the third level of insight, the student clearly sees the beginning, middle and end of each object noticed. For instance, the initial, middle and final phase of each abdominal motion is clear. He understands that objects arise one by one, and that only after the earlier object has ceased can a new one be known. At this level the student begins to see the impermanence, unsatisfactoriness and impersonality of mind and matter.

The imperfections of insight appear at level four. These pseudo-enlightenment experiences may fool the student into thinking he has reached a high spiritual level. Mindfulness, insight or equanimity can seem very strong. The student might feel joy, rapture, peace, or see a bright light. He may express resolute faith in the Buddhist teachings and wish to practice "even unto death."

Why are these pleasant experiences called "imperfections"? Not because they are inherently unwholesome. Like everything else, they are comprised of momentary, phenomenal blips—nāmas and rūpas. Even the joy is impermanent. But the meditator may become subtly

---

64. *Fundamentals of Insight*, p. 29.

(or grossly) attached to them. Many students fail to make a mental note of the lights or blissful feelings, believing the rule does not apply to those objects. Until letting go of attachment, the student can't progress to the higher levels of insight. Later, with the aid of his teacher or his own maturing understanding, he realizes, "The brilliant light, and the other things experienced by me, are not the path. Delight in them is merely a corruption of insight. The practice of continuously noting the object as it becomes evident—that alone is the way of insight. I must go on with just the work of noticing."[65]

It is a good sign if the student can see his desire to prolong the pleasant experience. A skillful meditator, "wisely reflects that that desire would not have arisen in him if he had actually attained a supramundane stage. So he concludes that this could not possibly be the path, and dismisses the illumination with a mental note."[66] As the student continues to note objects from moment-to-moment, he no longer regards the blissful experience as important or special. His focus now is only on the momentary arising and passing away of each phenomenon.

At this level of insight-knowledge (No. 4), clear comprehension (*sampajañña*) begins to replace momentary concentration as the chief support for mindfulness. It is clear comprehension that knows the difference between an ultimate object (nāma or rūpa) and a conventional one. Clear comprehension is able to distinguish, for instance, the pure phenomenon of motion from the concept "my leg" or "my abdomen." With the aid of *sampajañña* the meditator sees that each movement is an impersonal material phenomenon,

65. Mahāsi Sayādaw, *Progress of Insight*, p. 20. He also writes, "The meditator should not reflect on these happenings. As each arises, he should notice them accordingly: 'Brilliant light ... tranquility, happiness and so on.' ... Cherishing an inclination towards such phenomena ... and being attached to them, is a wrong attitude. The correct response that is in conformity with the path of insight is to notice these objects mindfully and with detachment until they disappear." *Practical Insight*, pp. 25–6. The meditator, Ven. Mahāthera Matara writes, should, "carefully make a mental note of all the imperfections of insight whenever they arise. Meditators who neglect this precaution, thinking: 'After all, these are good things,' will ultimately find themselves in difficult straits, unable to advance in meditation." *Seven Stages of Purification*, p. 39.
66. Mahāthera Matara Sri Ñāṇārāma, *Seven Stages of Purification*, p. 36.

not part of his self.[67] *Sampajañña* works together with mindfulness and wise attention. Although it is weakly present in the earlier stages, clear comprehension becomes pronounced beginning with the fourth level of insight.

When clear comprehension is strong, the student no longer has to label each object with a mental note to keep his attention from straying. Indeed, at times the quick succession of phenomena will be too fast to label. When that occurs, Mahāsi Sayādaw explains, the student should not attempt to name each sensation specifically; instead he should, "notice them generally. If one wishes to name them, a collective designation will be sufficient (such as "feeling," "knowing," etc.)" (*Practical Insight*, p. 23). At that time, rather than making the abdominal motions his primary focus, the meditator can simply be aware of whatever arises at the six sense doors with broader mindfulness.

A moment ago we mentioned some strategies to help the student gain insight more quickly. In addition to those techniques, he should understand precisely what to observe when meditating:

> The object of vipassanā meditation is a real object. It is not conceptual or imaginary such as shapes, forms, words or concepts such as man, car, house, flower and so forth … Real objects are things not conceived out by the mind; they are real phenomena with their own characteristics and qualities that are not relative. They exist whether we know it or not … One such object is the motion experienced by the mind at the body door.
>
> (Ven. Sujīva, *Wisdom Treasury*, p. 8)

The objects appropriate for insight meditation fall into four groups, called the Four Foundations of Mindfulness. They are: 1)

---

67. "To know the sitting position is *sati*; to know it is sitting rūpa is *sampajañña*." Tullius, *Vipassanā Bhāvanā*, p. 38. The fourth level of insight has two stages. The second phase of level 4 is called "final knowledge of contemplation of arising and passing away," which occurs after the student passes the imperfections of insight. See Mahāsi Sayādaw, *Progress of Insight*, p. 20. The student perceives nāma and rūpa clearly beginning with the latter phase of level 4. This should not be confused with level 1 in which he is merely able to distinguish them. In general, Just Seeing can occur from the second phase of level 4 through level 12.

body, 2) feeling, 3) consciousness and 4) mind-objects. They can be reduced to: material and mental phenomena (rūpa and nāma). In practice, however, we cannot always observe the correct object, especially in the beginning. Achan Sobin compares the work of noticing objects to a chicken pecking the ground for grain. Sometimes the bird gets the food, sometimes it doesn't.

Examples of rūpa are: the four bodily postures (experienced subjectively as tactile pressure or motion, including the abdominal motions); color; sound; scent; and flavor. Examples of nāma objects are: pleasant or unpleasant feeling; consciousness with or without greed, hatred or delusion; wandering mind; restlessness; lust; anger; and sleepiness.

Furthermore, the meditator should be aware that the present moment is comprised of two inseparable components, an objective phenomenon (mental or material) and a knower (again, not a self, but impersonal consciousness and mental factors).[68] It is impossible to be aware of an object without the mind—the knower—being present also. The mind is there when we see an aqua or ocher shape, because it's the mind that senses the hue. Conversely, consciousness can't arise without an object to know.

In order to apprehend the whole of the present moment, the student should observe the knower and the object simultaneously. His attention should be focused on both *as they arise together in the present*. That isn't to say he knows two objects at once. This distinction is important. He still observes one object at a time; but his attention includes the mind that knows the form. For any object *x*, the correct target for mindfulness is: *the act of knowing x*. What the student observes, in other words, is: the mind knowing the object. He sees this dual set on every occasion of noting.[69]

---

68. It is no contradiction that the first vipassanā-insight is "knowledge of the distinction between mental and physical processes." At this level the student knows there are two components to every moment: a form, which lacks consciousness, and the mind, which cognizes it. It is this budding analytical knowledge of discreteness that, when developed, ultimately destroys the perception of compactness (*ghanasaññā*). The latter, when not recognized as a concept, leads to attributing selfhood to beings and objects. Still, one cannot wholly separate mind and object because it's their very contact that forms the moment of experience.

69. See Mahāsi Sayādaw, *Satipaṭṭhāna Vipassanā*.

In the early stages of practice, the object is more distinct than the consciousness that knows it. But when clear comprehension grows strong enough, the student is able to see the knower as vividly—or more vividly—than the object. In vipassanā we aim to see the mind more than the body because the defilements' address is in the former. Although it is only a subtle shift of emphasis from observing the object *per se* to observing the-mind-in-the-act-of-sensing-the-object, the keys to the kingdom lie in those few degrees of difference.

Think of it this way: if the mind is a mirror, the object being known is the reflection. Just as you can't peel the reflection from a mirror, you cannot separate object and mind. (And yet, as everyone knows, reflection and mirror are not identical.) It's a matter of where you want to focus. It's a bit like the difference between looking in a mirror to check your hair and looking because you might buy the mirror. In the former case your focus is on the reflected image. You care about and identify with it.

But when buying a mirror, you aren't concerned with the beauty or ugliness of the reflected image. You inspect the whole object including the frame. Having ceased to care about the reflection's content, the mind dissociates from it. It matters only that the image is clear, not what it's an image *of*. This is akin to observing the mind more than the object. Although the reflection hasn't changed, you no longer care about the mare's nest it shows—you are only concerned with the picture's veracity, its lack of distortion. And yet, though indifferent to the content, you can't avoid seeing it. How could you appraise a mirror otherwise?

Likewise, in observing the mind itself, in tracking *knowing*, you cannot fail to be aware of an object at all times, because it's the nature of the mind to apprehend something. But the more important half of the duo is the mind, since greed, hatred and delusion reside there, not in the object. As insight increases you begin to perceive the mirror more than the reflection, with increasing subtlety.

In the early stages of meditation, objects are still experienced in terms of conventional meanings. When hearing a noise you think "dog" or "bird" instead of noting *hearing* or the phenomenon of sound. Or sometimes consciousness doesn't literally call out the name but you sense it buzzing in the background, like a fly trying to get through a screen. But now you may see an ordinary object— a cup, a shoe, a cushion—and not immediately recognize the form.

When hearing a sound you may not know if it's a bird or a rusty hinge. Indeed, you may not even identify it as a *sound*, as opposed to a sight. At mealtime you may not recognize what you are eating. Before you are only color-patches, not green beans or rice. Instead of chicken or cheese you taste an unidentified burst of sensation.[70] (New meditators may be surprised the first time they're aware of seeing a shape, hearing a sound, or tasting a flavor without recognizing it, but they probably won't perceive the object's dissolution clearly yet. Deeper levels of insight will gradually accompany the experience of Just Seeing, Hearing, Tasting, and so on.)

As you continue to note each sensation impartially, without clinging, the phenomena being noticed seem clearer but also more subtle and empty, like a jet trail that looks solid from a distance but proves less and less substantial as you move closer—only segments of mist continually breaking up. The sense of body, self and other conventions recedes into the background while the ultimate characteristics, long hidden in the shadow of ignorance, slide into the foreground. Instead of the everyday features, which serve to differentiate phenomena, one begins to notice what all objects and the perceiving mind have in common: their momentary nature, their lack of substance, their ceaseless changing.

A single abdominal movement, or the arc described by the foot when walking, which before corresponded to a single moment, might now consist of several moments arising and passing away very fast. Each one is a quick, impersonal streak, a dissolving line rushing through space, having nothing to do with the body or self. The student observes motion, as distinguished from the physical limbs. Motion is its own phenomenon, separate from the leg or stomach muscles. Whether the moving part is the arm, foot, or abdomen, the student perceives only flux—the impersonal, moment-to-moment flux of nāma-rūpa. ("If one cannot grasp the true nature of the phenomena", Mahāsi Sayādaw writes, "one is misled to the notion that what is rising and falling is one's own abdomen. 'It is my abdomen' is, after all, a delusion."[71])

---

70. Mahāsi Sayādaw writes, "Some meditators say as they were noting the phenomenon of tasting, they failed to recognize what kind of food they had been given." *Mālukyaputta*, p. 44.
71. *Bhara Sutta*.

Although pleasant and painful feelings still arise, they disappear as soon as they're noted. Past events no longer disturb the mind. When seeing something good to eat, the old leap of desire doesn't occur. No longer, during a meditation retreat, does a student yearn for the break when he can walk outside with a cup of tea. Preferences die down until he feels unmoved by pleasant or unpleasant sensations.

"If, when you see, you just see it; when you hear, you just hear it," the Buddha said, "... you will realize that the sense-objects you perceive have nothing to do with you" (SN 35:95). When you cease becoming emotionally involved in these sensations, it will be increasingly clear that sights, sounds and thoughts are neither you, part of you, owned by you, nor happening *to* you or within you. Motion, color and all the rest are neither inside nor outside of an "I"—just freestanding vibrations appearing in space.

Earlier we described the fifth level of insight, called "knowledge of dissolution." On reaching this watershed stage, the meditator sees mental and material phenomena actually dissolving from second to second. "As knowledge of dissolution gets sharper," Mahāsi Sayādaw writes, "the mind is able to appreciate that both the object seen and the seeing pass away at a tremendous pace. A meditator who contemplates dissolution may feel that mind-consciousness is fluttering as it dissolves into nothingness. The impression is so hazy that he or she might think that something is wrong with his or her eyesight."[72] (This condition is temporary, however.) As if he were crawling out of himself backwards, the meditator now sees dissolution not only in every object as he notes it, but in each unit of noting consciousness as well. In this way he disentangles himself, moment by moment, from the thicket of mental and physical formations.

The next three levels of insight (6–8) are marked by a profound disenchantment with all of life. Momentary phenomena appear fearsome, dangerous, then insipid and completely undesirable. This state is unlike the *angst*, boredom or depression of everyday

---

72. *Mālukyaputta*, p. 18. Elsewhere he says, "The phenomena show no sign and vanish rapidly ... In noting the rising and falling, etc., the meditator does not have a mental picture of the abdomen, the body, or the leg ... when he or she notes bending and stretching, he or she does not have an image of the hand ... He or she sees only the vanishing of the noting consciousness and the object of attention as disjointed units." *Sallekha Sutta*, p. 265.

life. It isn't caused by unfulfilled desires, but arises from an unbiased insight into the unstable nature of mind and matter. As long as he remains at this stage the student finds no delight in sensation of any kind. Even the most exquisite sight, sound, smell, taste, touch or thought seems disappointing. Having clearly seen the worthlessness of all mental and physical phenomena, the meditator exerts more effort to free himself and reach Nibbāna, which he now regards as the only happiness. This effort accelerates through the next two stages of insight (9 & 10).

As liking and disliking wane, equanimity waxes. At the next stage of insight-knowledge, called "equanimity about formations" (No. 11), the fearful aspect of mind and matter disappears. Formations no longer seem good or bad, pleasant or unpleasant. The objects that touch the meditator's mind, whether attractive or repulsive in conventional terms, appear to him neutral. In his mental response, too, he is "impartial and neutral toward all formations."

Now the meditator accepts the continuous pageant of phenomena without resistance or involvement, with no attempt to manipulate it. He is disinterested, yet fully aware. Mindfulness seems more fluid and natural. In fact, the student may not feel he is practicing at all. No longer is there a need to look for objects or direct the mind to them. The act of noting hums along on its own, as if powered by some machine. Objects and the knowing of them seem to arise by themselves, as if chucked out of some cosmic conveyor belt. Not only (the student sees) is noticing occurring by itself, but *in spite of* himself.

"In spite of" is significant. At times the student may deliberately try to think about something, but find himself unable to; the momentum of the observing engine won't "let" him. He may want to stop practicing and stand up, but when mindfulness overrides the volition he continues to sit.[73] It had never been his

---

73. Mahāsi Sayādaw explains, "The insight is so swift and clear that [the meditator] comes to know even the momentary sub consciousness in between the processes of cognition. He intends to do something, for instance, bending or stretching an arm, and he readily notices that intention which thereby tends to fade away, with the result that he cannot bend or stretch for some time. In that event, he should switch his attention to contemplating the occurrences at one of the six sense doors." *Practical Insight*, p. 28.

self practicing, he understands then, but the group of wholesome mental factors. Even mindfulness is impersonal—nonself.

Here a few words should be said about intention. The more we can see the subtle intentions lurking behind our thoughts and actions, the more we can peel off deeper layers of ignorance. As experience is gained in meditation, we gradually come face-to-face with the ego-construct. Hidden levels of volition motivated by desire, aversion and delusion are uncovered and brought into the light of the conscious mind. Instead of merely wanting to do away with suffering we might find, for example, we are practicing in order to subtly enhance the ego. The way to deal with these hidden agendas is to note them as we would any other object. We don't have to do anything else to them. Delusion is automatically dispelled when they are seen with mindfulness.

Even the wholesome intention to follow the meditation instructions should be noted. For example, when the intention appears, "Now I'll be aware of rūpa," that very mental event should be noticed. The desire to see impermanence or nonself should also be noticed, as should the desire for enlightenment. Experience is nothing more than a psycho-physical process of momentary, changing conditions. Our intentions, even about meditation practice, occur within that stream, not outside of it. In the ultimate sense they, too, are impersonal. As such they should not be regarded as *me*.

Someone might wonder, if desire must be dispelled in order to reach Nibbāna, isn't it self-defeating to meditate, since we do so out of a desire to be free? At first this seems a paradox. But we have to use desire skillfully to eliminate desire. There are unwholesome and wholesome desires, those that keep us in the loop of suffering and those that lead out to brightness. Wholesome desire must be used in the beginning or one wouldn't practice at all. The stages of insight can only be developed step by step. At the higher levels—but not until then—desire will be consumed by the very force of wisdom it helped develop. (We should understand that arahants, fully enlightened beings, still have volition (*cetanā*), but not desire in the sense of greed. Their actions are motivated by wholesome qualities such as wisdom and compassion.)

To return to our discussion of the levels of insight: when a student reaches the stage of equanimity about formations, he will rarely experience the joyful feelings of the earlier levels. Although he may have felt joy or rapture at the fourth stage of insight, "The higher levels of insight knowledge ... wherein the meditator sees only the passing away," says Mahāsi Sayādaw, "usually have nothing to do with joy."[74]

This might seem strange. If equanimity about formations is a more advanced insight, shouldn't it feel more joyful? A sensation, even an extremely pleasant one, that lasts only a split-second cannot be regarded as a cause for rejoicing. At the fourth level of insight the momentary disappearance of each mental-material blip is not yet clear. Yet by the time he reaches the stage of equanimity the meditator has become disenchanted with feelings, having seen their impermanence. For that reason he has, "abandoned exultation, delight and pleasure ... There is no longer great exuberance, gladness, happiness, or delight." Rather, "He dwells contemplating all *saṅkhārā* [formations] manifested in seeing, hearing and so on with complete equanimity" (Mahāsi Sayādaw, *Great Discourse*, p. 168). But that's not to say he feels dejected. On the contrary, this equanimity seems better than the pleasant feelings experienced at the lower levels of insight. If he continues to practice he will eventually reach Nibbāna, awakening. The Unconditioned, according to those who have touched it, is so superior to the joy of the lower insights that it cannot be compared.

Just as the desire to change posture may be cut off by mindfulness, so any emotion or attachment is automatically cut off, even the subtle attachment to insight-knowledge. When the mind is virtually free of clinging, the meditator will feel there is nothing worth getting excited about, not even the sudden realizations along the way. This is the beginning of a free mind.

Although we have been surveying the levels of knowledge in ascending order, practice rarely follows a consistent upward curve. While there is a gradual progression over months or years, within that larger framework most students advance, fall back and advance again many times.

Even at the higher levels of insight, mindfulness, concentration and clear comprehension fluctuate according to conditions and cannot be made steady by sheer determination. This fluctuation

---

74. *Sallekha Sutta*, p. 20.

applies not only on the macro level, from day to day or week to week, but on the momentary level as well.

For instance, within a thirty-minute practice session, a run of moments in which the student knows nāma-rūpa may be punctuated by a few moments of general mindfulness. (Or, more often, stretches of general mindfulness will be dotted with a few moments of knowing nāma-rūpa.) Even during a meditation retreat, a student might witness a quick alternation between, say, knowing sound or touch, and knowing the bark of a dog, his own hand, the branches and leaves outside the window—instances of ordinary mindfulness. The alternation between stronger and weaker *sati* and even outright distraction is par for the course.

Sometimes it is only when letting go of the fierce determination to be mindful that *sati-paññā* leaps forward, as was the case for Ven. Ānanda. After the Buddha's death, Ānanda, the Buddha's personal attendant, tried to attain enlightenment in time for an important Council of arahants. Having failed to reach his goal by the morning of the meeting he gave up his meditation, deciding to lie down and rest. In the split-seconds between sitting and lying down he attained awakening.

Most of the time we are merely sharpening the blade of mindfulness and wisdom so it will be keen enough, at some future hour, to cut through delusion in a few quick strokes. Even at the level of equanimity about formations (No. 11) it is no small feat to keep mindfulness and concentration steady for more than a couple of hours. Mahāsi Sayādaw explains:

> Nor [at this stage, No. 11] does he reflect in any manner. But if he does not develop sufficient progress of insight to gain the 'knowledge of the path and its fruition' [the first stage of enlightenment] ... within two or three hours, concentration becomes slack and reflection sets in. On the other hand, if he is making good progress he may anticipate further advance. He will become so delighted with the result that he will experience a fall ... In this way, some meditators progress and fall back several times. (*Practical Insight*, pp. 34–5)

The meditator can minimize these ups and downs by noting the thinking or anticipation, instead of following it. He should not become discouraged, no matter how many times he falls back. "In

spite of such fluctuation in progress," Mahāsi Sayādaw writes, "...
as soon as the five faculties (indriya) of faith, energy, mindfulness,
concentration and wisdom are developed in an even manner he
will soon ... realize Nibbāna" (ibid., p. 35).

The Sayādaw often uses the phrase "between sequences" or
"between moments of noticing" to express the idea that in between
individual acts of knowing bare phenomena, reflections or
thoughts can arise. This phrase is interesting for a couple of
reasons. The level of detail alluded to may remind us how wide is
the gulf between everyday attention and the awareness developed
in vipassanā, subtle in the extreme, an awareness that can detect
the thinnest slice of experience. It also reminds us that the work of
noticing objects occurs in clearly delineated units called
"moments" and that these moments, and the mental factors
accompanying them, can differ wildly from one to the next with no
transition between.

Having experienced a moment of strong mindfulness, the
meditator often expects the next instant to be the same. Or else
when practice is not going well he becomes dejected, believing the
slump to be a permanent state. But soon the student learns that he
cannot predict what will happen even in the next instant, cannot
know when mindfulness will lag or sprint forward. Although it is
certainly possible to cultivate mindfulness (if it weren't, why
bother to practice?), the microscopic shifts of the mental gears are
not amenable to direct influence; they are, again, nonself.

Several passages in *Practical Insight Meditation* are concerned
with the student's response to the thoughts that intrude between acts
of knowing nāma-rūpa. "While giving more attention to the bare
noticing of objects," writes Mahāsi Sayādaw, "the meditator must ...
also notice these reflections if they occur, but he should not dwell on
them" (p. 23). This passage is key. When a thought comes, even a
thought about the Buddhist teachings, the meditator, at the very
moment of having the thought, may not be engaged in bare
noticing. But the thought can immediately become the object of
awareness in the next moment. (What should not be focused on is
the content of the thought.) In that case the thought will fall away as
the momentum of noticing rolls on. But if the student fails to notice
the reflection he is likely to cling to it, in which case thinking will
continue unchecked and more desire, aversion and delusion arise.

On becoming aware of thinking, we shouldn't go back to find the spot where mindfulness was lost or try to reconstruct the links in the cognitive chain. We can't bring those thoughts back to acknowledge them. The longer we dwell on objects from the past, the more nāma-rūpas slip by in the present. Better to drop the whole tangle and turn toward the new Now.

Whether a thought is good or bad in conventional terms is irrelevant during vipassanā practice. Imagine two meditators: the first has many unwholesome thoughts, but lets them go right away. The second clings to wholesome thoughts about the Buddhist teachings. Which student is practicing correctly? The first. In everyday life, of course, it is better to have wholesome thoughts. But all objects have equal value during meditation.

In the ultimate sense, a thought is only a type of movement, a mental gesture, nothing more. We cannot control what kinds of thoughts arise. But we can do something about our response. Nothing should be clung to in vipassanā practice. Every thought should be let go as soon as it is noted.

In daily life, unpleasant thoughts seem solid and permanent, which is why they cause distress. But if you can step back from the content and regard thoughts as the temporary sensations they are, they will not have the power to disturb you. Thoughts will have no impact as they come and go like clouds through the mind.

When a meditator is aware of a thought early enough, it disappears. Then he realizes, "The thought was not in existence before; it appeared just now and disappeared at once. I have previously imagined thought to be permanent because I have not carefully observed it. Now that I have watched it, and seen it disappearing, I know it truly as it is, impermanent" (Mahāsi Sayādaw, *Great Discourse*, pp. 115–6).

As we said earlier, Just Seeing can't be forced. And yet a meditator aims to Just See. The apparent contradiction is only that: apparent. One can speak of Just Seeing as a method, if by that is meant the repeated effort to note whatever sight, sound or touch presents itself in the present moment. But the real thing takes you by surprise. It's like the moment of epiphany when you make an impossible catch on the field or play a tricky piano passage without a hitch. Although we try to watch nāma and rūpa as opposed to conventional realities, the meditator's only duty is to practice. When and where he succeeds depends—as ever—on conditions. But as long as he is practicing correctly, success is sure to come. The student should be assured that insight-knowledge will arise by itself, as the inevitable result of his effort. The Buddha guaranteed this.[75] But the effort doesn't call for overbearing force and gritted teeth. It's a matter of gentle persistence and repetition: persistence in the enterprise, repetition in bringing the mind back to the present, literally second by second—and it's all done with a light touch.

While engaged in everyday activities, as we said before, we often have to know concepts, whereas during meditation we try to know realities (nāmas and rūpas). Yet even during formal practice, "though we can try to be mindful all the time, we cannot always have 'realities' as objects" (Ven. Sujīva, *Wisdom Treasury,* p. 8). Although it would be unrealistic to expect, even during formal meditation, that we could notice realities continuously, no moment should be excluded. Experience keeps rolling toward us and all of it, including doubt about the teachings, the intention to be mindful, and even the stretches of distraction, can and should be subsumed under the broader, ongoing effort of noticing.[76]

Think of feeding paper into a shredding machine. We can insert the paper in single sheets or in stacks. It's the same with the machine of mindfulness. We can put a big or small chunk into the slot at once. Sometimes many individual acts of noticing will occur without break. At other times, ten minutes of fantasizing will pass before we realize it. But no matter how long it lasts, we still have to notice each lapse. We can't leave any paper sitting on the desk. The beauty of it is, as soon as we notice the lapse, that stack of experience drops into the machine. Small or large, it's all food for mindfulness.

"Sometimes," says Acharn Kor, "there's the intention to look and be aware within, but there come times when there's no intention to look within, and yet knowledge arises on its own" (*Looking Inward,* p.

---

75. The Buddha, in the Satipaṭṭhāna Sutta, said whoever maintains mindfulness without break for seven years, months, weeks or days (depending on his aptitude) will undoubtedly reach a level of enlightenment.

76. Nyanaponika Thera explains that mindfulness can be considered continuous as long as there is no *unnoticed* break. See *Heart of Buddhist Meditation,* p. 105.

48). The next level of insight happens in the second way. It doesn't take hours, days, or weeks, but split-seconds. In a single moment the student glimpses the dissolution of one nāma-rūpa. That dissolution is clearer and sharper than before, dramatically so, like seeing a firework burst. At the same time, the student clearly sees impermanence, unsatisfactoriness or nonselfness through direct insight. He is surprised at beholding something new.

The object does not have to be a sight. Any ultimate phenomenon will do. The *Dhammapada* says, "Those who perceive the arising and ceasing of mental and physical states, even though they live for a day, are far better than those who never see the arising and ceasing of mental and physical states and live a hundred years."

Mindfulness only sees the object; wisdom knows its impermanence, unsatisfactoriness, or impersonality clearly. Although each meditator perceives all three characteristics during the course of practice, at this high level of insight one quality becomes prominent. Which characteristic he sees depends on his temperament; but like the many facets of a crystal, all three qualities are aspects of a single truth.

The experience just described is the first of three or four moments collectively known as "insight leading to emergence" (No. 12).[77] Those few moments mark the end of mundane vipassanā knowledge. When we said it was enough to Just See for a few moments in a row, it was this insight to which we were referring. After the final moment in the series, according to the texts, the student knows Nibbāna for the first time.[78]

---

77. According to Mahāsi Sayādaw there may be as many as ten moments. See *Great Discourse*, p. 172.

78. The last mind-moment in this series is called "anuloma," meaning "knowledge of adaptation" (level 13 on the 17-stage model. Emergence and adaptation knowledge are usually grouped together. Mahāsi Sayādaw counts them as separate knowledges). Next comes a single mind-moment called "change of lineage," (*gotrabhū*) marking the transition from an ordinary person to a Noble One (No. 13). The student realizes Nibbāna in the moment called "Path Knowledge" (No. 14). Nibbāna is experienced again for two or three moments during "Fruition Knowledge" (No. 15). Once level 13 is reached, the next two insights follow immediately and inevitably. Last comes knowledge of reviewing (No. 16). (Nos. 13–16 correspond to 14–17 on the seventeen-stage model.)

In emergence-knowledge the quality of speed is even more pronounced than in the rapid vanishing of phenomena experienced up to that point (which began with the stage of dissolution). When equanimity about formations is fully developed, Mahāsi Sayādaw explains, the meditator will experience, "very fast-moving and distinct" insights. "There appears a special kind of knowledge which seems to occur very rapidly ... When this rapid vipassanā comes to an end, Nibbāna is realized" (*Great Discourse*, pp. 171–2).

Most meditators fall back to the stage of equanimity after they experience the first moment of emergence-knowledge. In that case wisdom and its supporting qualities are not yet strong enough to make the leap to Nibbāna. This type of student needs to cultivate mindfulness and wisdom further. However, the first taste of emergence-knowledge is a threshold of sorts, greatly increasing the meditator's confidence in the Buddhist teachings.

A meditator who reaches this stage is called "*culla sotāpanna*," meaning, "lesser streamwinner." This person usually cannot be reborn in the sub-human realms in his next existence or even, according to some, in the next three lifetimes. If he continues to meditate but does not gain enlightenment in his present existence, it is likely he will do so in a future lifetime.

After several moments of emergence-knowledge, the sticks burst into flame: the student realizes Nibbāna for a few consecutive moments. Again this sequence is said to be very brief, lasting, "just an instant, like the duration of a single thought of noticing." During the experience of Nibbāna, according to the Pali texts, nāma and rūpa cease. "Nibbāna ... is void of formations since it is the cessation of them." Wisdom consumes the lower fetters, which can never return to trouble the mind.[79] Afterward the mind returns to mundane consciousness and reviews what has occurred. That is the final stage of insight-knowledge (No. 16).

Even after gaining the first level of enlightenment, although a person has become a Noble One and can never revert to the status of an "ordinary worldling," his mindfulness and concentration continue to fluctuate somewhat. When a Noble student resumes

---

79. Mahāsi Sayādaw, *Progress of Insight*, p. 33; ibid. The fetters destroyed at the first stage of enlightenment are: 1) personality-belief; 2) doubt about the Buddhist teachings; 3) misplaced faith in rites and rituals.

vipassanā practice after the experience of enlightenment, Mahāsi Sayādaw writes,

> the bodily and mental processes appear to him quite coarse, not subtle as before at the time of the knowledge of equanimity about formations [No.11]. Why is this so? This is so because the knowledge present now has the nature of the knowledge of arising and passing away [No. 4]. For when the noble disciples ... resume the practice of insight ... the knowledge of arising and passing away usually arises at the beginning.[80]

In other words, after reaching the highest level of insight and becoming a streamwinner (one who has entered the stream to Nibbāna), a student may drop down to level four again. The Sayādaw explains further:

> The development of insight belonging to the higher paths is, in fact, not as easy as that of insight belonging to the fruition attainment already achieved by the meditator. It is in fact somewhat difficult, *due to the fact that insight has to be developed anew.* It is, however, not so very difficult as it was at the first time when beginning the practice. In a single day, or even in a single hour, he can gain the knowledge of equanimity about formations.[81] (Italics added.)

Becoming a streamwinner is the result of the student's previous effort. Like climbing four ladders, new effort must be made for each level of enlightenment. Hence, "insight has to be developed anew." The streamwinner, therefore, does not always remain at the stage of equanimity whenever engaged in meditation. He may have to build his way back up to it, whether that takes one hour or one day of practice. What does not fluctuate is the fact that he knows from personal experience Nibbāna is real; and he is guaranteed, within seven lifetimes, to reach it permanently. Whereas ordinary beings continue to cycle indefinitely through saṃsāra, never certain of obtaining a pleasant rebirth, the streamwinner has cut the circle. To do so is the goal of insight meditation.

---

80. Ibid., p. 34.
81. Ibid., p. 36. "Fruition attainment" refers to the realization of Nibbāna.

A celebrated pianist might perform the same piece splendidly one night and only passably the next. The moments of brilliance when he seems to surpass himself can't be willed. Even *he* can't say why he's better on Thursday than on Sunday. And yet, though no one can name the date, the stellar performance wouldn't occur at all without the years of training. So, too, the meditator can't predict when wisdom will arise, but it can flash forth at any time when the right conditions are assembled and waiting.

CHAPTER 7

Looking again at Seurat's print we notice something curious. The picture's two aspects—the park scene, and the impersonal dots—inspire opposing responses. Stepping back to view the painting from a distance we see that boats, people and trees sprout in a twinkling. Based on these distinctions we're ready to make comparisons, to say we like this but not that.

On the other hand, when we stand close and perceive only motes, no such preferences arise. How could they? The characteristics of one flyspeck are the same as any other and inspire no passions. It isn't the case that some specks are pretty and others ugly. Only when groups of them are corralled within the fence of a name do they seem to acquire differences and therefore provoke favoritisms. But it's the whole aggregate that creates the appearance of difference.

In the painting, a certain group of white dots represents a sail, another group a dog. But if we could "pluck" one speck from the sail and another from the animal, shake them like dice and fling them on the table—could we tell which was which? Where would the sailness of the sail-dot be then, or the dogness of the dog-dot? The identity is created in the viewer's mind only when one dot is positioned next to others. An individual speck has no inherent sailness or dogness.

In a similar way, the identity we attribute to objects and beings, even the complex identity we give to our "self", is ultimately an illusion propped up by relative meanings. When we stop mixing the past with the now and look at the immediate present by itself, one moment at a time, the attributes that distinguish one conventional Thing from another fall away, and all sense-impressions are experienced as empty phenomenal sparks, no more different from each other than two white specks in the painting.

Although we might like the sail in the picture and dislike the dog, that wouldn't be true of the specks *individually.* An infatuation for one white dot or dislike of another is inconceivable. So, too, is nāma-rūpa barren soil for attachment; nor can aversion build a case against such neutral bursts of phenomena that arise merely to pass away the same instant.

Isn't that the great secret of nonattachment? As soon as we confirm the conventional meaning of a thing, notions of good and bad have already crept in, at which point it's too late to be unattached. But if we can separate pure phenomena from the concepts and only observe the former, not only is it easy to sever attachment, it's inevitable, because it won't have a chance to form. Each nāma-rūpa sparks out terribly fast, long before the watching mind can pin a label on it.

When the blurring effect of delusion is removed we'll see this right before our eyes. When phenomena are perceived as they actually are, the beautiful moment doesn't differ from the terrible one. And although each moment of Just Knowing lasts only an instant, its value isn't lost; the moments add up. Linked end to end, they build our bridge to freedom.

It behooves us, then, to observe pure phenomena before the mind crowns them with names, labels wrongly suggestive of pleasure or pain. But trying to unknot a moment of attachment that has already passed only gets us more entangled. In the meantime another movement, sight or sound comes rushing up. Will we catch it, or will we keep thinking about the one that has already collapsed like paper in a flame?

Since the aim is to relinquish clinging and regard all objects impartially, do we have to suppress desire whenever eyeing a lovely form? Forcing an artificial response isn't the answer. If we could see forms clearly, equanimity would arise on its own. The aim of Buddhist mental training is to prevent craving and aversion from sprouting in the first place, by digging out their root. Were our behavior as perfect as a neatly clipped topiary, unwholesome thoughts—and, eventually, actions—would continue to emerge as long as we hadn't uprooted delusion.

In seeing forms for what they are—mere empty oscillations— desire, hatred and delusion wane. Grabbing a hot glass dish by mistake, we drop it instantly. When the mind truly picks up the present moment it lets go immediately. Seeing it fizzle out before our eyes, the letting-go is automatic. There's no thinking or intention involved. We see there is nothing there to attach to. Ultimately speaking, does it matter if the mirage is called "garden" or "garbage"? Either way, it evaporates before we can tag it as lovely, terrible, or anything else.

But what about those objects that are more or less neutral? What about the wall on which we hung Seurat's print, for instance? Looking at it we feel so-so, neither liking nor disliking it. Does clinging still arise? Although we feel no desire or aversion for neutral sights, seeing them isn't the same as beholding nāma-rūpa. When eyeing a wall we're still aware of it as a relatively permanent object. Rather than knowing a burst of whiteness that arises and dies in a moment, we cognize a Thing that stands for two or two-hundred years. Although the latter perception is true in the conventional sense, it isn't the ultimate reality. In daily life we tend to ignore neutral objects. And yet, although we can't like or dislike nāma-rūpa, it's impossible to ignore. When it's clear we are attentive as never before, because it's something we have never glimpsed in the vast inventory of conventional sights and sounds.

For those who experience ultimate truth, does the world become a plain of unvarying beige, all distinctions sanded out? Would we still know the milk from the coffee, the spouse from the sister, the wheat from the chaff? Don't worry. When someone points to a pen we'll still know it's called a "pen," not a "cup." The names will sit on the shelf ready to be taken down as we need them. Working and conversing go on as before, but with a difference: the mind will feel lighter when we're able to lift or drop the conventions as necessary. Objects don't disappear forever once we overcome them; but we'll move through our days free of the mental suffering that comes from attachment.

The fully liberated person, the scriptures tell us, still understands the conventions. When using conceptual consciousness he knows as well as anyone that a hawthorn white with blossom is more lovely than an alley strewn with garbage.[82] But even while knowing the beauty of the blooming shrub, his mind is void of preference. It is the *attachment* to beauty, the partiality to it, that dies out.

---

82. It is said that arahants conceptualize, but they do so without wrong view. An arahant knows when he is experiencing a concept and when an ultimate reality.

More important, an enlightened man or woman still recognizes ethical distinctions and lives accordingly. Having penetrated delusion doesn't mean one is lost in a realm of bare sensation in which actions have no moral significance. Whereas unliberated beings, if sufficiently provoked, are always capable of unwholesome actions such as killing and stealing, an enlightened person can never commit such acts no matter how extreme the provocation. Moreover, the ethical behavior of the latter is effortless, stemming from an innate purity of mind.

Whereas ordinary folk can only compare one pleasant sense-impression to another, knowing nothing which transcends that category, it is said that an enlightened person compares the most prized sensation to Nibbāna—and finds no contest. Our preferences for certain sights, touches and flavors would seem foolish to someone whose mind was free of delusion. Who could care about imitation beads who had a twenty-four-carat, genuine article? But we're like gullible children who stake their lives on baubles of no worth. Sense objects alternately excite or depress the ordinary mind. But the mind of an arahant can't be moved by the changing spectacle of good and bad sensations. Mahāsi Sayādaw writes, "When the meditator sees the complete extinction of all psychophysical phenomena that arise and pass away, he knows that it is the highest bliss. He knows, too, that compared with Nibbāna, the ever arising and vanishing phenomena are painful."[83]

Nāma-rūpas, the Buddha said, are impermanent, unsatisfactory, and impersonal, lacking in self. Dukkha *is* nāma-rūpa. Nāma-rūpa *is* dukkha. "Dukkha" refers to that which is unsatisfactory because it cannot last. Even what we hold most dear is impermanent, as momentary as the lights breaking on the surface of a river. And impersonality (*anattā*) means that no phenomena, including the nāma-rūpas we regard as "me," can be produced, extended or destroyed by the pressure of anyone's will. Impervious to influence, they only come into being when the right conditions arise together. Nāma and rūpa, having no intrinsic identity, cannot be defined as this or that conventional thing.

When one of these characteristics stamps its seal on the mind,

---

83. *Sallekha Sutta*, p. 153.

the impression remains. Previously one believed formations to be long-lasting and enjoyable, threaded through with identity and meaning. Suddenly everything is opposite from what it had been. But one isn't disappointed by the new findings. Does that seem paradoxical? One isn't disappointed because the very act of seeing those traits cuts the chain of attachment. With that, the machine of suffering stops. It is said that when the world rushes back we face it differently, as people who have been given a treasure that cannot be destroyed or lost.

How radically could a glimpse of ultimate truth change our perspective? An old story will illustrate. Once, a monk was walking on his morning alms-round when a well-dressed woman passed him on the road, heading toward her relatives' house. She had quarreled with her husband that morning. Passing the monk she smiled, revealing her teeth. What would you and I have seen as she smiled? A friendly woman? A detective might have noticed the way she looked back over her shoulder. (Was she being followed? And all those gold bracelets—were they stolen?) And what might an artist have seen? Perhaps the neat proportions of her face, or the shadows made by the folds of her sari, as he wondered how to render them in paint.

Did the monk see the same, looking at the woman? A few minutes later the woman's husband came running up the road. Spying the monk, he asked: "Venerable sir, did you see a woman go by on this road?" To which the monk replied, "Whether it was a man or woman that passed I noticed not; but only that, on this road, there goes a group of bones." How many degrees our perspective might revolve!

But perhaps we're thinking, "Who would want to see the world as a walking graveyard?" Do we imagine the monk is missing out on beauty? His perspective might seem antithetical to life, to the *joie de vivre* we cultivate and admire, and which we'd be almost ashamed not to possess. Perhaps it sounds terrible, or negative—or terribly negative.

But was it so to the monk? He might have asked us: "Who would be sorry to trade a string of plastic pearls for a rope of genuine ones?" Would he mourn the loss of the worthless beads? Or would he be overjoyed at having gained something of genuine value?

At the sight of the woman's teeth the Elder cracked the code. At that moment of penetration, realizing the non-worth of nāma-rūpa, the Elder became a fully enlightened one, having overcome all forms. Delusion was extinguished. He saw, we can presume, that what he formerly took for happiness was in fact only stress, void of anything desirable. And that which the world holds unpleasant—liberation from objects—he understood to be the highest good. Seeing those things, the last fetters fell away.

Ultimate truth is the extreme converse of conventional reality. We read in the *Saṃyutta Nikāya*:

> These [pleasant sense-impressions] are deemed "sukha" [happiness] by both gods and men. And when they cease to be they hold it woe. The dissolution of body-self to ariyans seems sukha. Everything the world holds good, sages see otherwise. What other men call "sukha" that the saints call "dukkha" [unsatisfactoriness]; what the rest so name, that do the ariyans know as happiness ... hereby are baffled they that are not wise ... Blindness is theirs, who cannot see the light. (3:12)

Although saṃsāra's canvas surrounds us, windows are everywhere. Even a glimpse of someone's teeth or a painting of a park might burst before the eyes, pouring the light of dhamma through the mind. It is said that those who persist in this path until knowing phenomena as they are will fall into the stream to Nibbāna, the stream that flows against the varied swell of color, sound, touch, taste, smell, feeling and thought that is the daily flood. Nibbāna, permanent happiness, is the fourth ultimate reality. Unlike nāma-rūpa it is unchanging, whereas here (in the conventional realm) time has rolled the room forward on its arc.

Although we can gaze at the Buddha-picture that hangs in this very hall, that isn't really seeing the Buddha. That kind of seeing is a synonym for blindness. The Buddha said, "Whoever sees the dhamma sees me; whoever sees me sees the dhamma" (ibid., 22:87). Sees, that is, nāma-rūpa arising and passing away, and then the unconditioned element, Nibbāna. Seeing this is truly eye-opening, as evinced by the stock phrase in the suttas, the words of those who have attained vision: "The dhamma has been made clear in many ways by the Blessed One, as though he were righting the overthrown, revealing the hidden, showing the way to one who is lost, holding up a lamp in the dark for those with eyes to see visible forms." The dhamma—that's what we must see if we would free ourselves from sorrow. Everyone, the Buddha said, is capable of seeing this. Everyone has the means to free him- or herself from dukkha.

Now the tea is cold. Darkness comes with a charcoal pencil to cross out the picture in the hall. And so it will do later, in the marble-floored museums, to the great paintings themselves, and the quiet rooms in which they hang. In time it will blacken the earth those rooms rest on and, in the end, the stars. A blank slate will await the next round. Yet how long have we turned away as billions of nāma-rūpas rose and set? So let us turn and know the present moment now. Who knows? *It* might be the one to forge an outlet, to cut a fissure leading out from dukkha's stream, toward the freedom that waits like an open sea.

APPENDIX 1:

The Perceptual Process in Detail

Earlier we mentioned a process whereby the mind leaps from seeing color to perceiving a pigeon, a plane, or any other thing. Working our way through this process will help us understand Just Seeing.

In normal perception, it seems that as soon as an object falls into our line of sight we recognize it. Seeing and recognition are simultaneous. And yet, the Buddhist teachings tell us, the simultaneity is a perceptual trick, a speed-of-light sleight-of-hand.

Examining consciousness more closely, we find it isn't a seamless flow. Instead it resembles a running movie. Although we perceive it as continuous, it's actually comprised of a series of discrete "frames," like a film. Each individual frame in the perceptual movie is called a mind-moment (*citta-kkhaṇa*).[84] In the ongoing show of perception, seeing always occurs several frames before recognition.

Or, to change the simile, we can think of the stream of consciousness as a series of trains. A train is not all of a piece but is comprised of individual cars. Likewise, a given train of consciousness is made up of individual moments.

For a normal act of visual perception to happen, several trains must occur. Under ordinary conditions we cannot distinguish the separate trains, let alone the cars that comprise them. This sequential act is perceived as a single event, as if the trains were

---

84. "Citta," meaning consciousness, sounds like "cheetah" and runs even faster. Nothing in the universe, the Buddha said, can match the mind for speed. In regard to the continuity of a series of mind-moments, Mahāsi Sayādaw writes, "Any two consecutive units of consciousness are separate but, since they belong to the same stream of consciousness, we speak of the same individual for the whole day, the whole year or the whole lifetime." *Dependent Origination*, p. 29.

telescoped in on themselves. But let us now stretch the series of trains and examine the separate cars.

When a visible form impinges on the sensitive matter of the eye—given the presence of attention and adequate light—it sparks off a series of mind-moments. Each mind-moment, as we said, is like a single car in a train. (However, a train of thought does not occur *in* the mind but *is* the mind. There is no perceiver outside of it. As each car in the mental train arises it constitutes, for that moment, the totality of mental phenomena.)

Those cars appear in a set order, just as actual train cars are arranged, not randomly, but in sequence from the first car to the caboose. Unlike real train-cars, however, only one mind-moment (*citta*) can appear at a time. As soon as one citta appears it falls away and triggers the next one in sequence until the train is complete. We cannot preempt any of the cars or alter their order. From this we learn that we can't control our own moments of consciousness, since it is impossible to leapfrog over any of the steps.

After the last car passes, another train of thought begins.[85] In one minute, thousands of trains flash past. It is due to this incredible speed, mimicking simultaneity, that we seem at once to think of many things, "from cabbages to kings." But in truth we can only know one object at a time. Other impulses wanting to push their way out must wait. While one train is passing, even the king must wait at the crossing.

The First Train: The Eye-Door Process

First, let's look at the individual cars that comprise what is termed an "eye-door process." An eye-door process is a series of seventeen mind-moments that occurs whenever you see something. It is one type of sense-door process (the others are the ear-, nose-, tongue- and body-door processes).

An eye-door process is the first train in an act of visual perception. It is normally followed by several more trains. Imagine that the object you're looking at is, conventionally speaking, a pigeon.

---

85. Between each train of thought several moments of subconsciousness, called *bhavaṅga* (literally, "life-stream"), occur. *Bhavaṅga* cittas also occur in deep sleep.

The Passive Phase

You don't perceive the pigeon immediately. During the first three cars the mind awakens from a sleep-like state (the *bhavaṅga*) and turns toward the color, the visible object. Thereafter, mind-moments four through eight perform the following functions, respectively: 4) adverting to the color, 5) seeing the color (the moment of eye-consciousness, *cakkhuviññāṇa*), 6) receiving the color, 7) investigating the color, and 8) determining the nature of the color.

This brings us roughly to the midpoint of the train, a pivotal point. The eighth car, determining consciousness, evaluates the object, deciding whether it is agreeable, disagreeable or neither. (But the mind does not yet recognize the form in conventional terms.) Since the entire train has seventeen moments, nine cars have yet to occur. Note that neither liking nor disliking has arisen yet. The eight mind-moments that have appeared so far are ethically neutral, neither wholesome nor unwholesome.[86] If mindfulness can intercept the process at the next car, then greed, hatred and delusion cannot arise in the train. If mindfulness fails to appear, delusion comes aboard. By then it's too late for mindfulness to join the current train. It must wait for the next.

During meditation practice itself, however, most of us cannot know exactly when one train of thought ends and another begins, or which mind-moment is being experienced. The ordinary person cannot perceive the thought-process with that degree of subtlety.[87]

---

86. These eight mind-moments are either resultants (cittas resulting from our previous good or bad actions) or so-called inoperative cittas. Being neither wholesome nor unwholesome, they cannot themselves generate what is called "kamma-result". The word "kamma" ("karma" in Sanskrit) means intentional action. Kamma and its results are explained in detail on pp. 96–7.

87. However, according to Mahāsi Sayādaw, when Just Seeing, an experienced meditator is able to distinguish individual trains as separate cognitive events. Individual cars, however, cannot be noticed by most students, although the process of enlightenment may be an exception: For the first time in the meditator's experience, several levels of insight (13–15) occur within a single train, in fractions of a second. Each knowledge lasts only as long as one, two or three cars, and the meditator may subsequently remember each insight distinctly.

Nor is such precision necessary. During vipassana practice we only have to keep returning our attention to the object arising in the present moment, over and over again. A theoretical grasp of the process of consciousness is valuable for giving a student more confidence in the method of insight meditation. But one shouldn't think that in practice each mind-moment can be identified with the degree of precision being used here.

To return to our train: As we said, mindfulness is able to intercept a cognitive process before delusion arises, at the same time preventing desire and hatred from appearing. In that case the entire train, not only that individual car, will be free of those factors.

Why is it so important to forestall delusion? Ignorance, or delusion, is the fundamental cause of unhappiness. (Although the terms "ignorance" (*avijjā*) and "delusion" (*moha*) overlap, as Achan Sobin explains, ignorance pertains to mental states in the past, delusion to the present moment when consciousness is receiving an object.) Whenever delusion is present, some degree of attachment and wrong view are, too—and so is suffering.

Delusion triggers craving and aversion by causing us to misperceive the objects appearing at the sense-doors. Because ignorance conceals their true nature, we regard phenomena that are completely unstable as permanent entities. Blind to the worthlessness of formations we habitually grasp at them, generating fresh kamma (intentional action) that leads to renewed birth. With birth comes further suffering and death (the cessation of birth is not death or nothingness, but Nibbāna). Thus we perpetuate the cycle of dukkha. The solution is to erase delusion, which in turn dispels craving and grasping. When craving is dispelled, suffering cannot arise.

In the previous paragraph we used the word "kamma" (in more familiar terms, "karma"). Let's consider for a moment the meaning of this word, since it comes into play during the next step in the perceptual train. Kamma, as we said, means volitional action—whether mental, verbal, or physical. The Buddhist definition of kamma is quite different from the popular sense of the word as fate or a kind of cosmic payback for a past act. The notion of fate has no place in Buddhist thought.

Volitional action is a causative force producing an effect. The effects, or results, are called "vipāka." Kamma-result takes the form of sensation: pleasant and unpleasant sights, sounds, tastes, touches, smells and mental objects—in other words, our daily sensory experience.[88]

Therefore, what in popular parlance is referred to as kamma, i.e., the good or bad events that seemingly befall us without reason, a Buddhist would call kamma-result. But these good and ill events result from our own past actions, not from fate or any external power.

Moreover, kamma, in Buddhism, does not apply only to momentous actions, egregious violations of the moral code such as killing or stealing—or, on the wholesome side, heroic acts like saving a life. According to the Buddhist teachings, we generate good and bad kamma all the time in the most trivial daily actions and thoughts. Because kamma is generated in the mind it does not require any outward expression to count.

Since thoughts accompanied by intention are kamma, they yield a result. But there are different degrees of kamma, producing weak or strong effects. The result of a single thought may be imperceptible, while the result of an act such as killing is usually very great. (That said, what makes an action kammically weighty is the strength of the intention. A man who accidentally takes a life does not reap the painful result of a man who kills intentionally.) Still, the kamma generated solely by thoughts cannot be discounted, for reasons we'll discuss in a moment. Now let us return to our train of thought, which we left at the point of determining consciousness.

The Active Phase

The perceptual process up to this point has been essentially passive. The first eight mind-moments are kammically neutral, meaning a person does not generate new kamma but only apprehends, in various ways, the form being presented.

After the determining *citta* (car No. 8) makes a decision about the color, it is succeeded by six or seven mind-moments called

---

88. Strictly speaking it is the *vipākacitta* (resultant mind-moment) that is the result of kamma, not the sense-object itself. But a *vipākacitta* must know—i.e., experience—an object.

impulsions (*javana*).[89] The impulsions constitute the active phase of perception. (As the Abhidhamma commentary explains, "*Javana* pertains to the active side of *present* existence, and determines the passive side of *future* existence."[90]) From the meditator's viewpoint, they are the most important cars in the train. The impulsions are the moments during which new kamma is generated, both wholesome and unwholesome. During those moments we respond to the form being perceived. The problem is, we often respond unskillfully, with craving or aversion. In feeling attracted or repelled by the sights and sounds appearing at the sense-doors, and acting upon those desires, the mind generates unwholesome kamma that perpetuates suffering.

Impulsions occur during every complete train of consciousness, whether that train is a perceptual act in which you see, hear, smell, taste or touch something (a sense-door process), or a so-called "mind-door" process in which you know a mental object. For any given train, it is only during these six or seven cars that new kamma is generated. It would be impossible, for instance, to make kamma at the moment of eye-consciousness (mind-moment No. 5, *cakkhuviññāṇa*).

Now we can understand the phrase "Just Seeing" more precisely. In terms of the Abhidhamma, Just Seeing means to interrupt a train of cittas with mindfulness at the first impulsion, thereby preventing unwholesome kamma from being generated in that train.[91] Just Hearing, Smelling, etc. should be understood in the same way.

As the Buddha told Bāhiya: "When you see, just see it." The John Ireland translation reads, "In the seen, there will be merely the seen." That is, there will be merely the visible object present, as opposed to the visible object plus the *kilesas* (mental impurities). The commentary states, just as eye-consciousness itself is free of greed, hatred and delusion, so should the following impulsions be free of those factors. Therefore, "merely the seen" means to have impulsions devoid of greed, hatred and delusion.

---

89. There are six or seven impulsions when the object is strong. See Nyanatiloka, *Buddhist Dictionary* p. 82.
90. Rhys Davids, *Compendium of Philosophy* p. 248.
91. Vipassanā-mindfulness is meant.

To intercept each cognitive process with mindfulness before delusion, aversion or craving arises is, according to Mahāsi Sayādaw, the essence of the Bāhiya teaching. "When one sees," he writes, "one must stop at the thought moment of determining and note all phenomena with mindfulness. It is the same as saying, 'When you see, you just see it'" (*Mālukyaputta*, pp. 16–7).

The word "determining" needs some explanation. For any sense-door process, the Sayādaw held that mindfulness appears at the moment of determining consciousness (mind-moment No. 8). The view that mindfulness can appear so early in the train is somewhat unorthodox, although at least one contemporary Abhidhamma teacher shares it.[92] The prevailing opinion is that mindfulness does not appear until the initial impulsion (car No. 9), as was stated earlier.

In any case, mindfulness can occur *no later than* at the first impulsion. That's because all seven impulsions are obliged to respond uniformly. The first one sets the pattern. As it likes, dislikes or feels indifferent toward the object, so do the other six. As the first impulsion is tainted with craving, hatred or delusion, so are the rest. But if the first is charged with mindfulness, so will the others be, automatically.

Whenever mindfulness is lacking, delusion is present during the impulsions, and the conditions for dukkha, unsatisfactoriness, accumulate. On the other hand, observing an object with mindfulness turns the compass needle toward awakening. When *sati* knows a sight or sound as it is, without the bias of delusion or craving, the meditator begins to generate the kamma that leads to the cessation of kamma, both wholesome and unwholesome. Each series of impulsions with mindfulness is another step on the path toward liberation.

By worldly standards, actions motivated by loving-kindness and other positive factors are wholesome kamma yielding a pleasant result, whereas actions accompanied by greed or hatred produce unpleasant effects. But the good result yielded by

---

92. Achan Sobin Namto. In a conversation with the author he explained, although mindfulness does not yet have the duty to stop delusion at the moment of determining consciousness, it is able to "adjust the object" at that citta.

wholesome kamma is temporary. In order to reach Nibbāna, which is permanent, we must stop the process of generating mundane kamma entirely, including the wholesome kind. This requires a type of kamma that is "neither black nor white." As the Thai teacher Ajahn Chah said, "The aim of the Buddha's teaching is to practice to create a type of karma that is beyond happiness and suffering and that will bring peace."[93]

Although many positive mental factors contribute toward liberation, it is mindfulness and wisdom that directly block delusion during the impulsions. As the blade that cuts the round of kamma, *sati-paññā* is of highest importance.

Knowing that our behavior has consequences, most of us try to perform helpful actions rather than harmful ones. We are most concerned with bodily actions, gestures others can see. But what of the consequences of purely mental action? What of the innumerable flickers of liking and disliking, hundreds per day, that are normally ignored? Perhaps we don't even regard these thoughts and intentions as actions. But whenever the distracted mind likes or dislikes an object we have performed an action, regardless of whether or not the body moves. Because attention and clear comprehension are weak, however, we don't notice the yearning that seizes the mind.

It may be difficult to understand why those flickers of wanting should concern us. Darting under the threshold of normal awareness, they seem innocuous even to their owners. But *are* they harmless? In Buddhism, as we said, volition is the most primitive form of action, and as such it has results that boomerang back on us.

That's not to say that by wishing something harmful on another (or ourselves) we'll incur it. To believe that would be superstitious. An anvil isn't going to drop on our heads for hoping, for a moment, so-and-so were out of the way. We won't become indigent for thinking of stealing a shirt, or struck down with illness for wanting dessert. If those things did occur it would not be due to a stray thought, but to a complex of innumerable conditions. The wise person takes a realistic view, granting his thoughts neither more nor less power than they warrant.

---

93. *Everything Arises, Everything Passes Away,* pp. 62–3.

However, the occasional thought becomes habitual when repeated. Repeated thoughts shape traits of character, and those tendencies can determine the circumstances of our next rebirth. Habit is a force to be reckoned with.

The wisps of liking and disliking have another effect: namely, the mental smog that accumulates in the mind as they go unnoticed over weeks, months or years. The fact is, whenever mindfulness is absent we continue to generate delusion, desire or aversion during the impulsions in each perceptual train. Each moment may be negligible in itself, but when generated millions of times daily the cumulative effect is impressive. Unless *sati* can check the situation, ignorance surrounds the mind in layers of distortion that block the light of dhamma, preventing us from seeing the Four Noble Truths.

According to the Buddhist teachings, these Truths appear clearly at the first stage of enlightenment. It is these four facts we must realize in order to reach the end of suffering. So it comes down to this: the way to be free of suffering is to prevent delusion from arising just long enough to glimpse the Four Noble Truths. How long is "long enough"? Only a few moments, if the supporting factors are there.

The slight drafts of preference that rustle the mind are not harmful in an ordinary moral sense. But they are unskillful for being tinged with delusion. Each intentional action prompted by delusion is a kammic "seed." And the fruit? Continued existence in saṃsāra—i.e., more moments of nāma-rūpa.

Incidentally, someone might wonder: if each moment of consciousness arises and dies in an instant, how can kamma, or qualities like the perfections, be accumulated? Each mind-moment is accompanied by mental factors, which may include wholesome or unwholesome qualities. Like consciousness itself, the mental factors of the present moment are conditioned by those which arose before. Say, for instance, a bird flies one hundred miles to a protected spot, lays an egg, and dies just before the egg hatches. When the chick is born it starts life from the new spot. It doesn't have to repeat the hundred-mile trip its mother took. Although the young bird is a different being from its mother, it is affected by the mother's past actions. Likewise, each new mind-moment is influenced by the previous ones. In that manner wholesome or unwholesome tendencies are strengthened. The memory of past actions is retained in the mental factor perception (*saññā*). *Saññā* arises and dies from moment to moment, too, but each fresh arising contains the memory of the mental continuum up to that point.

To return now to our train of consciousness, which we left at the point of the impulsions (the impulsions, remember, are those mind-moments during which new kamma is generated): after the seven impulsions pass, two mind-moments called "registration" occur. That completes the eye-door process.

To summarize what has happened so far: contact between the eye and a visible form triggered a train of consciousness called an eye-door process, made up of seventeen mind-moments. The first portion of the train consisted of eight kammically passive moments; the latter, of seven kammically active impulsions (plus two registrations, which are kammically passive).

The Seventeen Moments in a Sense-Door Process

Kammically passive	1) 1st Bhavaṅga
	2) 2nd Bhavaṅga
	3) 3rd Bhavaṅga
	4) Adverting to the sense-door
	5) Seeing the object
	6) Receiving the object
	7) Investigating the object
	8) Determining the nature of the object
Kammically active	9) 1st Impulsion
	10) 2nd Impulsion
	11) 3rd Impulsion
	12) 4th Impulsion
	13) 5th Impulsion
	14) 6th Impulsion
	15) 7th Impulsion
Kammically passive	16) 1st Registration
	17) 2nd Registration

During the eye-door process, consciousness only sees the visible form. It doesn't recognize it. Although seventeen moments have passed and you have come to the end of the first train, you have yet to reach the point of perceiving a pigeon. To do so will require several more trains of consciousness. (Remember, we are stretching into slow motion an experience that lasts only a microsecond. In real-time thousands of trains would pass in a flash).

The Second Train: the Conformational Mind-Door Process

After the eye-door process ends, a new train begins called a "mind-door" process. It is called "conformational" because it conforms to the previous sense-door process. The color-patch that was seen in the eye-process is already gone by the time the mind-door train begins. But perception (saññā) "photocopies" the form, and that copy becomes the new object. It approaches the door of the mind, triggering the new train of consciousness.

Although this second train has fewer mind-moments than the first one, the gist of the process is the same. Consciousness "wakes up" and turns toward the object. Thereafter, a series of impulsions arises, generating wholesome or unwholesome kamma; lastly, registration occurs. In the mere act of glimpsing a pigeon, dozens of mind-moments have rolled by already—and the process isn't over yet.

Even if mindfulness missed an opportunity in the previous train, there is still a chance for Just Seeing to occur here, at the first mind-door process. That's because the mind has not yet altered the form with conceptual knowledge. The object is still an ultimate reality, not a concept. Mahāsi Sayādaw states:

> When eye-consciousness has done its job [i.e., when the eye-door process has finished], mind-consciousness takes over, but it is still unable to distinguish the visible object as [for example] male or female. At this stage knowledge is still at the stage of ultimate realities (paramattha), as with the preceding eye-consciousness. (*Mālukyaputta*, p. 14)[94]

---

94. The phrase "male and female" is shorthand for any conventional concept. "Pigeon," etc., can be substituted.

Although the visual form itself has passed away, the copy cognized during the first mind-door train is a faithful reproduction. The Sayādaw writes, "If you fail to note the process of seeing just as it occurs [in the eye-door process], try to catch the first thought moment of mind-consciousness. One who can seize that moment and notice the absolute reality of form, may notice the dissolution of both the sense-object and the eye-consciousness at the moment of seeing (ibid., p. 29)."[95]

The same applies to hearing, smelling, tasting and touching. In regard to hearing, "Note with mindfulness the instant that you hear. (Note as soon as the process of ear-consciousness occurs or, failing that, note as soon as the process of mind-consciousness [i.e., the first mind-door process] occurs)" (ibid., p. 33).

To further refine our definition: Just Seeing (or Just Hearing, etc.), means to intercept a perceptual process with mindfulness, either 1) during the sense-door process itself, or 2) at the first mind-door process. In either case, mindfulness must appear at the first impulsion, no later.

But rarely are we mindful enough to seize the moment even at the first mind-door process. Consider a rock tossed into a pond: long after it has sunk out of sight the water ripples outward, continuing to register the impact. Likewise (unless mindfulness stops it here), the influence of an object impacting a sense-door does not stop after one series of mind-moments. Even after the object has dropped away, waves of influence reverberate through the mind, triggering many trains of thought (out of sight—*not* out of mind).

Trains 3–8: Recognizing the Object

Lacking mindfulness to stop the momentum, many trains of consciousness may be triggered by the original eye-contact. That brings us to the third train—the second mind-door process. At this point recognition begins to occur, in stages. Now the object of consciousness is no longer a visible form or its copy, but a concept.

---

95. The first thought moment of mind-consciousness presumably refers to the first impulsion. It bears repeating that, in truth, seizing the right moment cannot be done by desire, intention, or willpower, but occurs spontaneously when mindfulness is strong.

During this process the mind "grasps the object as a whole." It synthesizes into a unity the separate cars perceived in the two previous trains. It's like turning on a fan; the blades that were clearly separate when the fan was motionless now appear run together. As Mahāsi Sayādaw explains:

> Failure to note the object with mindfulness as it enters the mind door at the first moment of mind-consciousness prompts the arising of the second thought process. At this stage conceptual knowledge (*paññatti*) regarding the shape or form of the visible object begins to emerge, and it becomes firmly established at the third thought process. The subject is now able to distinguish the visible object as [for example] male or female. This clear cognition relates to both form and name, so concepts of name and form are conceived. (Ibid., p. 15)

If mindfulness fails to seize the moment before reaching the second mind-door process, there is a good chance, due to the concealing effect of ignorance, the real characteristics of the object will be distorted. Continuing from the end of the above citation, we read:

> This concept comes naturally in rapid succession during the second and third thought [mind-door] processes, but it is a concept gained through ignorance (*avijjā*), which conceals the true nature of the object. The commentaries say ignorance has the tendency to hide. The basic exercise in mindfulness exhorts a meditator to observe and note every time he or she comes face to face with the (ultimate) realities, before ignorance creates the concept. (Ibid., p. 15)[96]

What is the true nature that ignorance conceals? Impermanence, unsatisfactoriness, and impersonality. The purpose of insight meditation is to purify the mind of delusion and other unwholesome mental factors. These impurities, Mahāsi Sayādaw explains, only gain real strength beginning with the second and third mind-door trains. Hence the importance of stopping short with mindfulness before that point.[97]

---

96. This does not apply to arahants since they have eliminated delusion. Other Noble Ones and experienced meditators can also know a concept without delusion, although not invariably.
97. See *Great Discourse*, pp. 74–5.

Even after completing the second mind-door process, one still has not fully identified the form in conventional terms. At least five more trains must be set rolling in order to recognize the pigeon.[98] From this point forward every additional train will originate at the mind-door.

The functions of the next five trains (and note we are speaking of entire trains here, not individual cars) are: 1) recognizing the color 2) grasping the entity 3) recognizing the entity 4) grasping the name, and, finally, 5) recognizing the name.

The entire perceptual process looks like this:

Just Seeing Possible
{
1) sense-door process (17)
2) conformational mind-door process (12)
}

Conceptual Knowledge
{
3) 2nd mind-door process (grasping object) (12)
4) 3rd mind-door process (recognizing the color) (12)
5) 4th mind-door process (grasping the entity) (12)
6) 5th mind-door process (recognizing the entity) (12)
7) 6th mind-door process (grasping the name) (12)
8) 7th mind-door process (recognizing the name) (12)
}

The numbers on the right represent the individual cars in each train. Adding them together, we find that roughly one-hundred moments of consciousness may be involved in an ordinary perceptual act.

In summary, seven or eight trains must wend their way through the fog and it's only then, as the last one pulls out, that a pigeon is perceived. Yet in arriving at the object's name we have moved away from the original experience. Paradoxically, the more trains that pass—the longer you think about the object—the farther you travel from the pure color that was seen in the eye-process.

Whenever a fresh series of unwholesome impulsions goes over the same object, even if you're only *remembering* that form, more delusion, desire or hatred is stirred up. You may find that you recall some words or images again and again until they stick in the mind. "When you fail to stop short at seeing, hearing, etc.," Mahāsi Sayādaw writes, "your mind will cling to those passions, and

---

98. According to Ledi Sayādaw. See Bhikkhu Bodhi, *Manual of Abhidhamma*, p. 164.

whenever you recall those sense-objects they will again arouse lust, anger, and delusion." On the other hand, "When we note the phenomena of seeing, hearing, smelling, tasting, touching and thinking as each of them occurs, we will realize their true nature, and with this realization we can exterminate craving together with its supporter, delusion."[99]

Every time you see something, the same process of seventeen mind-moments occurs. Millions of thought-trains are triggered by sights and other sensations every day. The only way to prevent delusion from being generated in those trains is with mindfulness. But, again, it is only during the latter half of a perceptual train that mental impurities can be activated and strengthened. The mere act of seeing, smelling or touching generates no kamma.

Whether you are looking at a shape called "pigeon", "plane", or anything else, the moment of seeing[100] always occurs with the same type of consciousness, the citta called "eye-consciousness" (*cakkhuviññāṇa*). Furthermore, the thing seen is always the same kind of phenomenon: color (*rūpayatana*). The eye can't see sound, taste, or smell. Hearing- and smelling-consciousness require other objects in order to arise.

The eye's aperture can't admit such things as birds or planes. Because the eye-door can accept only one kind of guest, the different details of visual forms—their distinguishing shapes and patterns—are, ultimately speaking, irrelevant. From the absolute standpoint, the characteristics of one color-patch are identical to those of any other, the only difference being they occur in different moments.

The unit of consciousness (citta) that sees a particular image has no function other than to see at that moment. Instantly it dies. It does not persist to hear a sound, feel a touch, etc. It cannot even form the thought "I am seeing". That thought, if it occurs, is carried out by subsequent cittas, each of which is also highly specialized and inconceivably brief. Nowhere in this process can we find an enduring meta-consciousness aware of broader chunks of experience across time. As Mahāsi Sayādaw remarks, most people

---

99. Mahāsi Sayādaw, *Bhara Sutta.*
100. "Moment of seeing" refers to the actual citta of eye-consciousness here (car No. 5), not the entire eye-door train.

believe, "It is the same 'I' who sees as that which hears and touches ... But the meditator who is watchful of these phenomena knows that ... every act of seeing, hearing, touching and knowing is a new arising" (*Great Discourse*, p. 123).

Perceiving a pigeon, we realize now, is not the same as seeing a visible form. Seeing happens during an eye-door process, whereas knowing a pigeon is a conceptual act that occurs after the fact of seeing, during several mind-door processes.

Visual perception is only one kind of sense-door process. Every time a sound, smell, taste, or touch brushes against its respective sense-door (ear, nose, tongue or body) it sets off a protocol like the one described above. The only difference is that in place of eye-consciousness you have a moment of hearing-consciousness, smelling-consciousness, tasting consciousness, or body-consciousness. And whenever you know a mental object, the stream of consciousness must follow the order for a mind-door process.[101]

After you recognize the pigeon, the perceptual process starts over. The mind becomes aware of a new object—a new sight, sound, smell, taste, or touch—arising at one of the sense-doors. The process is so quick that in one second you can recognize hundreds of sense-impressions.

In summary, in regard to one act of perception, Just Seeing, Hearing, Smelling, Tasting, or Touching can occur during the sense-door process or the conformational mind-door process, but not in a subsequent mind-door process. Strictly speaking, staying in the "present moment" in vipassanā refers to being mindful at these early stages of the perceptual process, during which realities can be experienced as they actually arise and vanish. Therefore, Just Seeing, etc., is the same as knowing the present moment.

The recognition phase of perception, in which you identify the object by its conventional name, can also be defined more precisely now. Recognition happens in stages, beginning with the second

---

101. However, it is said that in the cognitive series that occurs during enlightenment, the path-moment is immediately followed by a fruition consciousness (its resultant) in the same train of cittas. In this case the seven javana cittas are not functionally identical as they would be in a mundane process of consciousness.

mind-door process (the third train). It consists of any trains of consciousness subsequent to the first mind-door process. It is during these trains of thought that conceptual knowledge develops.

* * *

As you may recall, part of the instruction to Bāhiya and Mālukyaputta was, "When thinking, just think." But isn't a thought already conceptual? What does it mean to Just Think?

The gist of the Bāhiya instruction is to note, with mindfulness and clear comprehension, every object as soon as it comes into contact with consciousness—at the earliest point of entry through one of the perceptual doors. By so doing we prevent the mind from clinging to sense-impressions. Up to now, when speaking of concepts we have chiefly been referring to concepts that arise subsequent to a sense-door process—i.e., to those ideas that are a direct consequence of seeing, hearing, touching, smelling or tasting something in the present (as when you see a shape in front of you and recognize it as a cup, for example).

But the mind itself is the sixth perceptual door. Some objects enter the mind-door directly, without passing through the eye, ear, nose, tongue or body-door first. When a conceptual object enters the mind-door in an independent process, we have a different situation than when it enters subsequent to a sense-door process.[102]

Even in its most primitive form, a thought which arises spontaneously at the mind-door is already a conceptual object. What should you do? Ignore it or observe it? First, it should be

---

102. The mind-door is the *bhavaṅga*, life-continuum. "An independent mind-door process occurs when any of the six objects enters the range of cognition entirely on its own, not as a consequence of an immediately-preceding sense door process." Bhikkhu Bodhi, *Manual of Abhidhamma*, p. 164. The John Ireland translation of the *Bāhiya Sutta* reads, "In the cognized will be merely what is cognized." The phrase "in the cognized," the commentary explains, refers to the adverting citta of a mind-door process. An independent mind-door process is probably meant. As we know, the Bāhiya instruction moves from seeing to hearing, etc. Since hearing entails a new sense-door process, not a continuation of the previous eye-process, it is likely "in the cognized" also applies to the initial process of a new cognitive series.

understood that this type of concept may be triggered by different conditions than a thought based on a sense-door process. The latter type of thought—let's call it a "sense-concept"—must be fashioned over the course of several trains, as we saw in the example of the pigeon. It is the end-stage of a string of processes occurring in the (relative) present.

Although the pigeon is conceptual, the original object of perception (the object that initiated the series of trains) was not a concept but a visual form. Seven or eight trains had to pass from the time the color entered the eye door until a pigeon was perceived. The object in the first train was a rūpa. The object in the last train was a concept. At some point in between the object was, figuratively speaking, switched (the switch occurred at the third train).[103]

In a kind of existential shell game run by ignorance, we start with an ultimate reality and end with a conceptual one. In failing to notice the rūpa that initiates the process, we assume the concept had been there from the outset. We mistakenly take the pigeon to be the original object. Knowing only the conceptual pigeon, we remain ignorant of the rūpa that triggered the series of trains in the first place.[104] (A meditator, however, may realize the concept was not the original object.)

As we have seen, during any perceptual event there are two chances for mindfulness to intervene and note the bare sense-datum: at the sense-door process and the first mind-door process. However, if someone is only aware of a pigeon, his mindfulness (at the time) was not strong enough to stop short at either train. It only caught the tail-end of the perceptual act, by which time the color-patch had already been replaced by a concept.

A thought or concept that enters the mind door spontaneously, on the other hand, may arise due to any of a number of reasons, these having little or nothing to do with the relative strength of mindfulness. Some of the factors that can trigger an independent mind-door process include: "the power of kamma, disturbance of the bodily humors, the influence of a deity, comprehension,

---

103. The rūpa in fact disintegrates at the end of the sense-door process.
104. The rupa in this case would of course be a color-patch. On the way in which "consciousness plays conjuring tricks," see Mahāsi Sayādaw, *Great Discourse*, p. 77.

realization," and so on.[105] No matter how mindful you are it isn't possible, for instance, to prevent a thought arising if it's due to the power of kamma. Here there is no possibility of mindfulness intercepting the mental current before the concept is formed, since the original object is already conceptual. The thought should be accepted as nonself, something over which you have no control, noted and immediately let go.

The advice against conceptualizing is intended to prevent us from superimposing concepts onto the original object. But when the original object is a concept to begin with, you need only note it as soon as it appears and cease to think about it further. As long as you don't conceptualize the concept you are still following the Buddha's injunction to Bāhiya. "With the range of mental objects too," Mahāsi Sayādaw writes, "you will just stop short at the point where mind-consciousness arises without formulating concepts" (*Mālukyaputta*, pp. 21–2).

But during meditation you shouldn't try to figure out whether a given thought resulted from a lapse in mindfulness or arose spontaneously at the mind-door. In either case the method is the same: note the thought as soon as you're aware of it, just as you would note any other object, without adding *more* thinking. As Mahāsi Sayādaw explains, "Any idea must be noted as soon as it is formed so that the inclination to defilements has no opportunity to arise. When the defilements cease, kamma and results also cease" (ibid., p. 57).

As we mentioned before, it is not only the object that arises and passes away, but the knowing consciousness itself. The experienced meditator, observing the act of thinking, does not get engrossed in the content of the thought. When a thought appears he automatically focuses on the *knowing*. By refraining from getting involved in the content, whether pleasant, violent, intelligent or stupid, he sees the impermanence of each moment of consciousness.

What the meditator experiences is the pure sensation of thinking, which is nothing more than a mental movement. "As he or she notes it like this," Mahāsi Sayādaw writes, "no attachment arises. In other words, mindfulness dispels lust or passion. In such circumstances consciousness just occurs, it does not go beyond

---

105. Bhikkhu Bodhi, *Manual of Abhidhamma*, p. 164 (citing Ledi Sayādaw).

that. This is in accordance with the instruction ... 'when you know, just know it'" (ibid.).

* * *

Let's take another look at the phrase "stopping short," or, as Mahāsi Sayādaw sometimes calls it, "stopping the mind." The Bāhiya formula, according to Bhikkhu Ñāṇananda, "consists in *stopping-short* at the level of sense-data without being led astray by them."[106] (Italics Ñāṇananda's). As should be clear by now, when you stop at the bare sense-datum the mind can't drum up craving or aversion to lead you into suffering.

"Stopping the mind" does not mean consciousness literally ceases. Think of stopping a stream of water with your hand. Invisible pressures still force the water out of the hose, but it doesn't travel far. Although it spurts out here and there between your fingers as it hits the palm, the water can't shoot out in an eight-foot arc to the edge of the yard. It stays right here in your hand. In the same way, although the pressure of past kamma causes mind-moments (cittas) to issue forth, when *sati* interrupts the momentum of craving, consciousness stays right here in the present. Mind-moments continue to form just the same, but they don't run out in a long stream to the past or the future.

When an object enters one of the sense-doors it begins what could be called a "cognitive thread," a consecutive series of trains triggered by that sense-impression.[107] In order to know a pigeon, as we saw, eight trains were needed. If we may be excused an awkward shift in metaphor: those eight trains together constitute one cognitive thread. (Earlier we strung cars together to make a

---

106. Bhikkhu Ñāṇananda, *Concept and Reality,* p. 31.
107. Rhys Davids (*Compendium of Philosophy,* p. 34) refers to, "complex groups of processes." There is a causal relation that obtains among certain groups of consecutive trains, and in order to speak of them conveniently we have coined the term "thread," which refers to an initial sense-door process (or an independent mind-door process) plus its consequent processes. Only consecutive processes are meant. If the mind returns to an object *x* after an intervening sense-door process that cognized *y,* the new cittas regarding *x* would not be counted as part of the original thread. Within one thread there are still bhavaṅga cittas between each train.

train of consciousness. Now we'll string trains together to make a thread.)

But the mind doesn't always stop after eight trains. Unlike a single train of consciousness, a thread has no determinate length.[108] In daily life eighty or eight hundred trains may be triggered in sequence by a single sense-datum. In the absence of strong mindfulness, delusion and desire might keep adding to a thread until a more compelling object commanded the attention. Yet as soon as mindfulness intervenes, that cognitive thread ends. There are other conditions that might trigger the start of a new cognitive thread. Yet one thing unique about mindfulness is its power to break the force of delusion and craving that compels the ordinary mind to dwell on certain thoughts obsessively, even when they generate suffering.

"Since sense-objects fail to generate defilements in the meditator," Mahāsi Sayādaw remarks, "there is no reason for the meditator to recall them [the objects], and so defilements are discarded" (*Mālukyaputta*, p. 23). In essence, stopping short and letting go are the same.

But what happens to consciousness after it stops short? What does it know? There is always another object ready to be received at one of the sense-doors. The mind starts over with a new sight, sound, smell, taste, or touch. Another thread begins. With sati in charge, the mind turns to the next phenomenon lightly, free of the hidden agendas of desire, with no sense of looking for something better or trying to grasp the new form. The mind simply receives the next sensation.

For any cognitive thread, if mindfulness can interrupt the flow of consciousness at the first mind-door process, according to Mahāsi Sayādaw, the second mind-door process need not occur. That thread ends there. When the mind stays in the immediate present with bare attention it will not go beyond the first mind-door train. This is stated repeatedly in the *Mālukyaputta* discourse, as in the following passage concerning hearing: "The process of

---

108. While the commentary states that roughly seven consequent processes must occur in order to recognize a sense-datum, it seems there is, in theory, no upper limit for the number of such processes. As Rhys Davids explains, in an actual case of perception each stage of conceptualization may be repeated many times (ibid., p. 32).

mind-consciousness [i.e., the first mind-door process] is only aware of the sound, and concept has not yet been formed. If you can note this with mindfulness, apperception ends here."[109]

Although the term "stopping short" can be used in a more general sense, in Mahāsi Sayādaw's *Mālukyaputta* it means to begin a new thread after the first mind-door process has passed (or after the sense-door process, in which case the entire thread would only be one train long). On this definition, the pattern of trains when Just Seeing would look something like this:

Diagram 1

1. *SD*	2. CMD	3. *SD*	4. CMD
[*rrrrrrrrrrrrrrr*]	[rrrrrrrrrrr]	[*rrrrrrrrrrrrrrrr*]	[rrrrrrrrrrr]
5. *SD*	6. CMD	7.*SD*	8. CMD
[*rrrrrrrrrrrrrrr*]	[rrrrrrrrrrr]	[*rrrrrrrrrrrrrrr*]	[rrrrrrrrrrr]

r=a citta that knows a rūpa
SD=a sense-door process
CMD=conformational mind-door process
Italics indicate the beginning of a thread

Here four separate threads occur within eight trains of consciousness. Whenever sati stops short, a new thread begins.

---

109. *Mālukyaputta*, pp. 32–3. Even the first mind-door process, Mahāsi Sayādaw says, need not occur if sati can intercept the cognitive stream at the sense-door process. "When one sees, one must stop at the thought moment of determining and note all phenomena with mindfulness" (ibid., pp. 16-7). Here he must be referring to a sense-door process, since there is no determining citta in a mind-door process. See also ibid., pp. 23 & 33, and *Great Discourse*, p. 78. Achan Sobin, in an interview with the author, said, "It is absolutely possible for sati to stop short at the sense-door process." He explained, whereas a mind-door process would always follow a sense-door one in ordinary perception, the case is different when vipassanā-nana is strong. However, these are minor philosophic points, and the ultimate aim of studying Abhidhamma is to experience realities directly. At times the knowledge gained through meditation may not correspond to a particular theoretical detail we've learned. As Dr. N.K.G. Mendis said, "What is important is the essence; it is this that we should try to experience for ourselves."

Compare this to a series in which a sense-concept is known. In the latter case all eight trains belong to one thread:[110]

Diagram 2

1. *SD*	2. CMD	3. MD	4. MD
[*rrrrrrrrrrrrrrr*]	[rrrrrrrrrrr]	[cccccccccccc]	[cccccccccccc]
5. MD	6. MD	7. MD	8. MD
[cccccccccccc]	[cccccccccccc]	[cccccccccccc]	[cccccccccccc]

r=a citta that knows a rūpa
c=a citta that knows a concept
SD=Sense-door process
CMD=conformational mind-door process
MD=Consequent mind-door process
Italics indicate the beginning of a thread

Not all conceptualizing is motivated by unwholesome mental factors, of course. As we know, conceptual thought is necessary for ordinary tasks like cooking a meal, writing a letter, repairing a faucet and so on. If the obligations to work and family are done with right understanding, the thoughts involved will be wholesome.

Even an arahant (fully enlightened being) might think conceptually for a long time, as when giving a dhamma talk. But in contrast to the ordinary worldling, his or her mind would be under no *compulsion* from the defilements to do so (nor would he misunderstand the concepts he was experiencing). The obsessive power of craving that can force the ordinary mind to spin a thread out longer and longer is entirely lacking in the arahant. The motivation to conceptualize might come instead from the mental factor wisdom or compassion. A sight or sound does not impact

---

110. According to *Compendium of Philosophy* in a real case of ordinary perception the mind might repeat the sense door process and its conformational mind-door process many times before moving on to the stage of conceptualizing the object. In the early part of this process, therefore, there might appear a series of trains like those in Diagram 1. Yet this would differ from a case in which the mind, due to the influence of *sati-paññā*, experienced a consecutive series of different sense-door processes, each having a new object, with no interruption from conceptual thought.

the mind of a Holy One such that a long series of trains *must* be generated about it.

* * *

Experience is an ongoing barrage of colors, sounds, and other stimuli bombarding the open sense doors. When we're unmindful of these phenomena they trigger countless thoughts involving liking and disliking. The impulsions in these thought-trains, and the verbal and physical actions that spring from them, are new kammas that keep the wheel of suffering turning. But if *sati-paññā* (mindfulness and wisdom) can stop delusion, even for a few moments, the benefit is greater than any worldly gain.

Fortunately, the practice of observing the mind is as simple as the theory is complex. Reviewing the theory of consciousness, as we have done here, can help us understand the reasoning behind Just Seeing. But as we said earlier, at the moment of eyeing a color-patch we cannot know—nor do we need to—whether we're on mind-moment five, nine or fourteen.[111]

In practice you only have to note an object the instant you become aware of it. Then stop there. Don't describe it or judge it. You don't even have to give it a name. Immediately drop that phenomenon and go on to the next one. Know and let go.

This procedure cuts off the mind's tendency to wander, since consciousness can only receive one object at a time. And because the incoming flow of forms never stops, some new object will ever be rocketing toward you. You will never find, having dropped the last object, you are hanging in space with nothing to observe.

The good news is, you don't have to cut off all unwholesome impulsions or stop them permanently. (Only the arahants have entirely ceased generating ethically weighty impulsions, both unwholesome and wholesome.[112]) It is said that beholding even one moment with wisdom, as it arises and vanishes, is a boon that will carry over into future lifetimes. And perceiving ultimate phenomena

---

111. Although ordinary people cannot know this, it is said the Buddha was able to, as are some Noble Disciples.

112. When arahants cognize an object they still experience seven impulsions; but those cittas are inoperative, neither wholesome nor unwholesome, and do not produce kamma.

clearly for a few moments may be enough to realize enlightenment. Although it isn't easy to intercept the train of consciousness with mindfulness and wisdom, it is certain that anyone who practices vipassanā to the end of the path will do so, calling a halt to the engine of suffering. Although we may spend lifetimes preparing the ground for awakening, the actual experience, the Noble Ones say, occurs in a flash. Having entered the stream to Nibbāna, there's no turning back. The endless cycle of future lives in saṃsāra, which formerly had no visible end, is cut off. Someone who enters the stream can have no more than seven rebirths.

To summarize the process of seeing: color is experienced through the eye-door first. At that point you don't see a being or a thing, don't know if the object is called "pigeon" or "plane." Thereafter a photocopy of the color is sent to the mind-door. Over the course of several trains of consciousness (all mind-door processes now) the mind evaluates, remembers, and recognizes the form, creating a conceptual entity. Every time an additional mind-door process recalls the object with liking or disliking, more kamma is generated. In order to reach Nibbāna one must cut off the process of generating kamma, both wholesome and unwholesome. This is done by repeatedly stopping short, with mindfulness, at bare seeing, hearing, smelling, tasting, touching and thinking.

The Buddha said: "Mālukyaputta! When you have nothing to do with the sense-objects that you perceive, you will get no foothold on them" (SN 35:95). As Mahāsi Sayādaw explains, "When a meditator lets go of craving and egoistic views, releasing himself from the ideas of 'I,' 'Mine,' or 'My self,' he cannot get stuck in sense-objects."[113] Understanding that there is no self behind the ongoing show of sense-impressions, the meditator will cease to get involved in it through liking, disliking and clinging.

By following the Buddha's instruction to Mālukyaputta and Bāhiya, we, too, can attain liberation. "Looking at a visible object, a meditator just sees it and just feels that he sees it, without conceptualizing it. With this, suffering ceases. One who practices in this way is said to be near to Nibbāna" (SN 35:95).

---

113. *Mālukyaputta*, p. 24.

APPENDIX 2:

A Meditation Exercise

[Note: These instructions are not meant to substitute for the guidance of a qualified teacher. Anyone serious about insight meditation should eventually find a teacher who can offer individualized counsel.]

During meditation you will eventually be able to notice sights, sounds, smells, tastes (in mindful eating), touches and mental objects as soon as they appear, but this can't be done in the beginning. Instead of deliberately trying to notice all these sense-data we train mindfulness by focusing mainly on tactile impressions, which include sensations of bodily movement. In this exercise you'll watch the in-and-out movements of the abdomen that happen as you breathe. This is in accord with the Bahiya teaching to Just Know touches.

Sit on the floor with your legs crossed, the right foot resting on the left thigh. If this position is uncomfortable you can sit tailor fashion or use a chair. Those who are ill or disabled can do the exercise lying down.

If you choose a sitting position, place your hands in your lap, palms facing upward, the right hand on top of the left. If doing the exercise lying down, place your hands on your abdomen, one on top of the other, or at your sides. Your eyes may be open or closed, but we recommend that beginners close them.

Direct your attention to the abdomen, an inch or two above the navel. Find the point that seems clearest to you. Don't actually look at the spot. Just place your attention there. The point should lie along the vertical midline of the body.

As you breathe in, the abdomen expands; as you breathe out, it contracts. In meditation these movements are called, respectively, "rising" and "falling." They never cease to alternate as long as you live.

As the abdomen rises, observe the motion from beginning to end. When it falls, do the same. That's all there is to it. Just keep watching the rising-falling movements. You don't have to do anything to them. Simply know the movements without judging or describing them.

Restrict your attention to what is occurring in the *immediate present moment*. Don't think about the past or future—don't think about anything at all. Let go of your worries, memories and plans. Empty your mind of everything except the movements occurring right now. But don't *think* about the motions; just *know* them with bare, impartial attention.

Keeping your mind on the movements may not be as easy as you think. Be patient and don't judge yourself, even if your mind wanders out often. Remember, you are learning a new skill. When learning to play the piano, for instance, you wouldn't expect perfection right away. You shouldn't expect it in meditation, either. Don't get discouraged if your progress seems slow. As long as you stick with the practice, results are sure to come.

Beginners should label the abdominal movements with a mental note (see pp. 59–60 for a full explanation of mental noting). As the abdomen expands, say the word "rising" in your mind. As the abdomen contracts, say "falling." Continue to note *rising, falling, rising, falling*, from one moment to the next.

Only say the mental note one time per movement. During the rising motion, for example, you would say the word "rising" once, stretching it out to last as long as the inhalation. Ninety-percent of your attention should be on the movement instead of the label. The aim in vipassanā is to know the object itself, not the word.

The mental note should coincide with the motion. Sometimes you might catch yourself saying "falling" after rising has begun, or vice-versa. In that case you are no longer knowing the present moment. Just start again by noticing what is actually happening *now*. If it is difficult to perceive the rising-falling motions, put your hands on your stomach.

Focus on the movement itself, not the abdomen. Bodily motion is felt subjectively as a sensation of pressure, which keeps changing from second to second.

The abdomen should not be visualized. In this exercise you merely watch the movements. Be sure to breathe naturally; don't try to control the breath in any way.

Resist the temptation to comment on the movements: "That falling motion lasted longer than the previous one. That rising movement wasn't as clear as the others," and so on. Simply know each movement with bare attention and then let it go. There's no need to verbalize or describe your experience.

The rising-falling motions are impersonal phenomena. Regard them with a detached, scientific attitude. An archer uses a target for practice. The objects used in meditation are targets for the arrows of mindfulness. Rising-falling is a moving target for mindfulness.

The rising-falling motions show themselves for the mind to know. They are rūpa (material form). It is nāma (the mind) that knows them. The mind—what you call "*your* mind"—is not a self, but an impersonal faculty whose function is to be aware of things.

Sounds, Smells, Sights

In this exercise the rising-and-falling motions are the primary meditation object. Nevertheless, other objects should be noticed as they arise (it is to be expected, however, beginners will have many gaps in awareness). For instance, when you hear a dog bark, note the bare sound, labeling it "hearing" (don't name it specifically as "dog barking"). Then return your attention to the primary object. When aware of a fragrance, say the mental note "smelling" for a moment or two, then go back to noting rising-falling. You don't have to identify the scent.

Your eyes will usually be closed during this exercise, so you won't have much occasion to see. But sometimes you might want to open the eyes if concentration becomes too strong. Or you may want to change posture, in which case you will probably open the eyes. When aware of color, just note the bare sensation of seeing for a moment or two, labeling it "seeing," then return to the primary object. It doesn't matter what the image is in the conventional sense. (Remember, the mental notes are said silently at the moment of perceiving the object, not added on afterwards.)

Wandering Mind

When you realize the mind has strayed from the present moment, note "thinking," then return your attention to the rising-falling movements. Don't get upset or judge yourself when the mind wanders away. To do so will only cause more moments to be lost, taking you farther from the immediate now. You don't have to ask, "How long have I been thinking? When did I stop knowing the rising-falling motions?" Those are more thoughts, and while thinking them you are still not observing rising-falling. If you become aware of thinking in the middle of a chain of thoughts you should try to let go at that point, leaving the story unfinished. Resist the temptation to follow a train of thought to its conclusion. (There is never a conclusion to thinking.)

Pay no attention to the content of a thought, whether good or bad. You don't need to feel guilty when unwholesome thoughts come. During vipassanā practice all objects, whether pleasant or unpleasant, wholesome or unwholesome, are regarded as equal. Eventually you will see what is common to all phenomena, including thoughts—their lack of staying-ness. Whether good or bad, thoughts are impermanent. They last only a moment before dissolving.

It is important to understand how to observe thoughts correctly because, as Mahāsi Sayādaw explains, thoughts and tactile sensations (especially the sensation of movement when observing rising-falling) are the most frequent objects of contemplation. Even painful thoughts should be noted and let go of, as should thoughts about meditation or the Buddhist teachings. When nothing else presents itself to be noticed, your attention should always revert to the rising-falling motions.

Itching and Other Unpleasant Sensations

As you observe the recurrent rise and fall of the abdomen you may feel an itch somewhere. Before scratching it you should observe the sensation, saying the mental note "feeling" or "itching." Often the itch will disappear on its own. If it does not, continue to watch it impartially. Desire will probably arise—desire to be rid of the itch. Label it with the mental note "wanting" or "desire."

If the itch persists and you must scratch it, do so according to the step-by-step technique:

1) Note the desire to be rid of the feeling, saying the mental note "desire".
2) Before moving your hand, note "intending to move".
3) Move your hand slowly and mindfully to the itchy spot, noting "moving".
4) Begin to scratch, noting "moving" or "scratching".
5) Move your hand back, saying the mental note "moving".
6) Place the hand in your lap, noting "placing". Now you are back to the original meditation posture.
7) Note the pleasant feeling that has replaced the unpleasant one, labeling it "feeling" for two or three moments. Notice if liking arises for the good sensation. If it does, label it with the mental note "liking" or "desire".
8) Resume watching the rising-falling motions.

Whether a feeling is pleasant, unpleasant, or neutral, be sure to note any desire that arises—the desire to get rid of the sensation or prolong it. Desire is a separate phenomenon from the feeling.

Pain

Don't automatically shift the body when you feel pain. Observe the sensation first. But if the pain becomes severe you should change your pose. It is not correct for beginners to grit their teeth and "tough it out." Only advanced meditators can observe severe pain effectively. It is too heavy for a beginner's mindfulness to lift.

On the other hand, you shouldn't change position at every little twinge or tingle. Don't give in to desire easily. Progress will not come without the patience to bear many unpleasant feelings. Only change position if you really cannot tolerate the pain and it is interfering with mindfulness.

If you decide to change position, follow the step-by-step technique:

1) Observe the sensation for a few moments.
2) Note the desire to be rid of the pain, trying, if you can, to isolate desire from the pain itself.
3) Say the mental note "intending to move".
4) Slowly move the body into the new posture, noting "moving". Break the entire action into several smaller

movements, stopping at the end of each one. This creates clear objects for mindfulness.

5) Note the pleasant feeling that has replaced the pain, labeling it "feeling" for a moment or two. If liking arises, label it "liking", or "desire".

6) Resume watching the rising-falling motions.

Everyone is biased when it comes to feelings, grasping at the pleasant and avoiding the painful. This deep-seated bias is called "attachment". The harm of attachment is (among other things) that it prevents us from seeing the impermanence of feeling.

In vipassanā we observe both pleasant and unpleasant feelings impartially in order to see their impermanence. The technique of noting objects as they arise prevents the mind from reacting to pleasure or pain according to habit. By repeatedly observing sensations with bare attention the true nature of feeling is revealed, and our attachment to it decreases. According to the teaching of cause and effect (Dependent Origination), desire is the cause of suffering, and desire springs directly from feeling.

Emotions

Strong emotions may sometimes arise during meditation. This is no cause for alarm. Although emotions are no more nor less important than other objects, they can be more difficult to observe. When an unpleasant emotion such as anger arises, don't try to suppress it. Nor should you look for a better object. Because the emotion is the truth of what is occurring in the present, it must be noticed. But don't let yourself get caught up in it. The correct approach is the Middle Way, without either liking or disliking. Have the attitude, "Here is just another object for mindfulness to observe." Separate your self from the emotion and observe it with scientific detachment.

Whether an emotion is pleasant or unpleasant, a beginner should label it with an appropriate mental note, such as: *fear, depression, joy, anger, peace, anxiety,* or simply, *emotion.* Confusion about the teachings or the meditation technique should be noted as *doubt* or *confusion.*

A fire reflected in a lake cannot burn the water. Neither can emotions disturb the mind when you don't get involved in them.

Don't identify an emotion as your self. The fear or anger is not you, only an impersonal phenomenon. Mentally pull back from the emotion and turn your awareness around to observe it. When in the grip of a negative emotion we tend to believe it will never end. But emotions are no more permanent than thoughts. With continued practice you'll find that you only have to wait and any emotion, whether pleasant or unpleasant, is bound to change. It might come back, but even so it passes away again.

Sleepiness

As with everything, sleepiness should be observed whenever it arises. Mentally note it as "sleepiness." If it does not disperse after a few moments of noting you can try these skillful antidotes: open your eyes, practice walking meditation,[114] turn up the lights, or splash your face with cold water. Cooling the room may also help. An excess of concentration can cause sleepiness.

Practice the rising-falling exercise daily for at least ten minutes, or as long as one hour. If you want to practice longer than an hour, alternate the rising-falling exercise with walking meditation.

Although no one can say how long it will take, with regular, correct practice insight will gradually arise by itself.

---

114. Instructions for walking meditation may be found at http://www.vipassanadhura.com/howto.htm.

APPENDIX 3:

Crossword Puzzle of Pali Terms

Fill in the Pali terms that match the descriptions.

Across

1. Wise or skillful attention; similar to everyday awareness but more systematic and sustained (p. 57).
2. Greed (p. 8).
3. Impulsions. The phase during the latter part of a perceptual process in which wholesome or unwholesome kamma is generated (p. 98).
4. Unsatisfactoriness; one of the three characteristics of all conditioned phenomena (p. 3).
5. This term has many meanings, one of which is the true nature of realities, both conditioned (nāma-rūpa) and unconditioned (Nibbāna). It also refers to the Buddhist teachings. (p. 29, n. 29).
6. Freedom from greed, hatred and delusion; the extinction of suffering; the goal of vipassanā practice (p. 3, n.1).
7. Ultimate reality, as opposed to conventional truth (p. 16).

Down

1. Clear comprehension (p. 57).
2. Delusion (p. 8).
3. Impermanence; one of the three characteristics of conditioned phenomena (p. 30).
4. Volitional action through body, speech or mind (p. 96).
5. Nonselfness; the quality of being impersonal, insubstantial and not amenable to control; the third of the three characteristics (p. 44).
6. Hatred (p. 8).
7. The type of meditation called "insight," that aims at seeing reality as it is (p. ix).
8. Mind-and-matter as they arise together from moment to moment (p. 17).
9. Matter; form (p. 16).
10. Mind (consciousness plus mental factors); mental phenomena (p. 16).
11. Mindfulness (p. 57).
12. Consciousness (p. 93, n. 84).
13. Round of rebirth (p. 33).

Answers:

Y	O	N	I	S	O	M	A	N	A	S	I	K	A	R	A
				A		O	N					A			N
				M		H	I					M			A
	D			P		A	C					M			T
L	O	B	H	A			C					A			T
	S			J	A	V	A	N	A						A
	A			A		I		A			R				
N				N		P		M		D	U	K	K	H	A
A				N		A		A			P				
M				A		S		-			A				S
A		S				S		R							A
	D	H	A	M	M	A		U				C			M
		T				N		P				I			S
	N	I	B	B	A	N	A	A				T			A
												T			R
P	A	R	A	M	A	T	T	H	A	-	S	A	C	C	A

APPENDIX 4:

Nāma and Rūpa Chart

NĀMA	RŪPA	KNOWER	OBJECT
MENTAL PHENOMENA (CONSCIOUSNESS & MENTAL FACTORS)	MATERIAL PHENOMENA (COLOR, SOUND, SMELL, TASTE, TACTILE FORM)	THE MENTAL FACULTY THAT KNOWS AN OBJECT	A PHENOMENON THAT IS KNOWN
KNOWER OR OBJECT	ALWAYS OBJECT	ALWAYS NĀMA	NĀMA OR RŪPA

BIBLIOGRAPHY

References to Pali sources use the Pali Text Society's original numbering. The *Saṃyutta Nikāya* is abbreviated in the text as SN. I have used the Mahāsi Sayādaw translation of Māluṅkyaputta Sutta, with slight alteration of syntax, except where noted. When quoting from other suttas I have mainly used the Pali Text Society translation.

Anālayo, Bhikkhu, *Satipaṭṭhāna: The Direct Path to Realization*. Kandy: Buddhist Publication Society, 2003.

Ayya Khema, *When the Iron Eagle Flies*. New York: Penguin Books, 1991.

Bodhi, Bhikkhu, ed., *A Comprehensive Manual of Abhidhamma*. Kandy: Buddhist Publication Society, 1993.

Bodhi, Bhikkhu (tr.), *The Connected Discourses of the Buddha: A New Translation of the Saṃyutta Nikāya*, 2 vols. Boston: Wisdom Publications, 2000.

Boriharnwanaket, Sujin, *Realities and Concepts*. http://www.abhidhamma.org/sujin3.htm, 2000.

Buddhaghosa, Bhadantcariya, *The Path of Purification*. Kandy: Buddhist Publication Society, 1991.

Chah, Ajahn, *Everything Arises, Everything Passes Away.* Boston: Shambhala Publications, 2005.

Kor Khao Suan Luang, Tan Acharn, *Directing to Self-Penetration*. Kandy: Buddhist Publication Society, 1985.

Kor Khao Suan Luang, Tan Acharn, *Looking Inward*. Kandy: Buddhist Publication Society, 1991.

Kor Khao Suan Luang, Tan Acharn, *Reading the Mind: Advice for Meditators*. Kandy: Buddhist Publication Society, 1993.

Mahāsi Sayādaw, *Bhara Sutta*. Rangoon: Buddha Sāsana Anuggaha Organization, http://www.dhammaweb.net/mahasi/book/Mahasi_Sayadaw_Bhara_Sutta.pdf, 1980.

Mahāsi Sayādaw, *A Discourse on Dependent Origination*. Bangkok: Buddhadhamma Foundation, 1999.

Mahāsi Sayādaw, *A Discourse on Hemavata Sutta*. Middlesex: Association for Insight Meditation, http://www.aimwell.org/assets/hemavatasutta.pdf, 2003.

Mahāsi Sayādaw, *A Discourse on Mālukyaputta Sutta*. Middlesex: Association for Insight Meditation, 2003.

Mahāsi Sayādaw, *A Discourse on the Ariyavatta Sutta*. Middlesex: Association for Insight Meditation, 2002.

Mahāsi Sayādaw, *A Discourse on the Sallekha Sutta*. Middlesex: Association for Insight Meditation, http://www.aimwell.org/assets/sallekhasutta.pdf, 2006.

Mahāsi Sayādaw, *The Great Discourse on Not Self*. Bangkok: Buddhadhamma Foundation, 1996.

Mahāsi Sayādaw, *Practical Insight Meditation*. Kandy: Buddhist Publication Society, 1971.

Mahāsi Sayādaw, *The Progress of Insight: A Treatise on Buddhist Satipaṭṭhāna Meditation*. Kandy: Buddhist Publication Society, 1994.

Mahāsi Sayādaw, *Satipaṭṭhāna Vipassanā*. Accesstoinsight.org, http://www.accesstoinsight.org/lib/authors/mahasi/wheel370.html, 1995.

Matara Sri Ñāṇārāma, Ven. Mahāthera, *The Seven Stages of Purification and the Insight Knowledges*. Kandy: Buddhist Publication Society, 1983.

Namto, Achan Sobin, *Wayfaring: a Manual for Insight Meditation*. Kandy: Buddhist Publication Society, 1979.

Ñāṇananda, Bhikkhu, *Concept and Reality in Early Buddhist Thought*. Kandy: Buddhist Publication Society, 1971.

Nyanaponika Thera, *The Heart of Buddhist Meditation*. Kandy: Buddhist Publication Society, 2005.

Nyanatiloka, *Buddhist Dictionary: Manual of Buddhist Terms and Doctrines*. Kandy: Buddhist Publication Society, 1988.

Randall, Richard, *Life as a Siamese Monk*. Bradford on Avon: Aukana Trust, 1990.

Rhys Davids, C.A.F., ed., *Compendium of Philosophy: Being a Translation From the Original Pali of the Abhidhammatta Saṅgaha*. London: Pali Text Society, 1910.

Rhys Davids, C.A.F. & Woodward, F.L. (trans.), *The Book of the Kindred Sayings (Saṃyutta Nikāya translation)*, 5 vols. Oxford: Pali Text Society, 1999.

Shattock, Rear Admiral E. H., *An Experiment in Mindfulness.* London: Rider & Company, 1958.

Sujīva, Ven., "Shoot for the Moon," reprinted in *Wisdom Treasury: Uncommon Essays on Buddhist Mindfulness Meditation*, Sister Dharmapālī, ed., 1996. (Self-published pamphlet.)

Tullius, Frank, ed., *Vipassanā Bhāvanā.* Chonburi: Boonkañjanaram Meditation Center, 1988.

Of Related Interest

A COMPREHENSIVE MANUAL OF ABHIDHAMMA
Bhikkhu Bodhi, General Editor
This is the classical introduction to the study of Abhidhamma, the Buddhist philosophy of mind and mental processes. The work contains a translation of Acariya Anuruddha's Abhidhammattha Sangaha along with the Pali text and a detailed explanatory guide to this ancient philosophical psychology. A long introduction explains the basic principles of the Abhidhamma. Includes 48 charts and tables.
BP 304S   426 pp.

THE PROGRESS OF INSIGHT
A Treatise on Satipaṭṭhāna Meditation
Mahasi Sayādaw
The meditation master charts the entire development of insight meditation to its culmination, with emphasis on the advanced stages. Translation and notes by Nyanaponika Thera.
BP 504S   64 pp.

MODERN BUDDHIST MASTERS
Jack Kornfield
This is one of the most valuable books in print on Theravada Buddhist practice, bringing to the reader the precise instructions of twelve great meditation masters, including Mahasi Sayādaw, Achaan Chah and U Ba Khin. With lucid introductory chapters and photos.
BP 507S   321 pp.

THE REQUISITES OF ENLIGHTENMENT
Ledi Sayādaw
This treatise by the great Burmese scholar-monk analyzes the thirty-seven modes of practice in which the Buddha summed up the way to enlightenment. It offers not only a wealth of information on the Dhamma, but also a forcefully reasoned and stirring appeal to earnest endeavour towards the goal.
BP 412S   138 pp.

THE HEART OF BUDDHIST MEDITATION
Nyanaponika Thera
A modern Buddhist classic, translated into seven languages. With the combined powers of deep personal insight and clear exposition, the author conveys the essential principles making up the Buddha's way of mindfulness.
BP 509S   224 pp.

SATIPAṬṬHĀNA
The Direct Path to Realization
S. Analayo
This book offers a detailed, thorough textual study of the Satipatthana Sutta, the foundational Buddhist discourse on meditation practice. This book is of great value both to scholars of early Buddhism and to serious meditators alike.
BP 422S   332 pp.

AN UNENTANGLED KNOWING
Lessons in Training the Mind
Upasika Kee Nanayon
(Acharn Kor Khao-suan-luang)
An inspiring collection of discourses by one of the foremost woman Dhamma teachers of modern Thailand. The teachings are direct and uncompromising in their honesty.
BP 515S   176 pp.

THE DISCOURSE ON THE ROOT OF EXISTENCE
The Mulapariyaya Sutta and Its Commentaries
Translated by Bhikkhu Bodhi
This profound and difficult discourse of the Buddha aims at exposing and eliminating the concept of the ego at its most fundamental level. The commentary offers a detailed explanation of the sutta while a long introduction investigates the text's meaning and its implications for philosophy and psychology.
BP 210S   90 pp.

Prices according to latest catalogue (http://www.bps.lk)

THE BUDDHIST PUBLICATION SOCIETY

The BPS is an approved charity dedicated to making known the Teaching of the Buddha, which has a vital message for all people.

Founded in 1958, the BPS has published a wide variety of books and booklets covering a great range of topics. Its publications include accurate annotated translations of the Buddha's discourses, standard reference works, as well as original contemporary expositions of Buddhist thought and practice. These works present Buddhism as it truly is—a dynamic force which has influenced receptive minds for the past 2500 years and is still as relevant today as it was when it first arose.

For more information about the BPS and our publications, please visit our website, or write an e-mail, or a letter to the:

Administrative Secretary
Buddhist Publication Society
P.O. Box 61
54 Sangharaja Mawatha
Kandy • Sri Lanka
E-mail: bps@bps.lk
web site: http://www.bps.lk
Tel: 0094 81 223 7283 • Fax: 0094 81 222 3679